WIRED FOR PURPOSE

Why HUMANITY is the BIGGEST DIFFERENTIATOR in a DIGITAL WORLD

What 30 Years in Business Taught Me About People, Progress, and Possibility

Aaron Strout

Published by Captain of Books (www.captainofbooks.com)

United States of America

ISBNs
Paperback ISBN: 979-8-234-02484-8

TABLE OF CONTENTS

"*Wired for Purpose* is Aaron's reminder that in a world sprinting toward AI and automation, humanity is still the sharpest edge you've got. Drawing on three decades of experience, he shares candid stories, practical rituals, and hard-earned lessons on gratitude, steady leadership, and building relationships that actually compound.

It's part field manual, part love letter to long-game leadership—and a compelling case that the future belongs to the most human among us."

— Ann Handley, CCO, MarketingProfs and WSJ best-selling author

"After years of investing in digital health, I've learned that the most important breakthroughs don't start with technology — they start with how leaders show up for people. *Wired for Purpose* resonated with me because it affirms that gratitude, calm judgment, and human connection aren't soft ideas in healthcare; they are the foundations of success. At a time when AI is reshaping what's possible, this book is a reminder that progress only truly matters when it improves lives."

— Lee Shapiro, Chairman of the American Heart Association, 7Wire founder and Healthcare investor

"Wired for Purpose is the rare leadership book that understands what's at stake in today's healthcare and technology landscape. Aaron brings a truth-telling clarity, a human-first mindset, and a bias for action that our industry desperately needs. His blend of gratitude, connection, and rational optimism offers a refreshing antidote to burnout and noise. This is a field guide for leaders who want to build trust, drive real impact, and elevate humanity in a digital world."

— Geeta Nayyar MD, MBA, WSJ best-selling author of *Dead Wrong*, Chief Medical Officer and Technologist

"Some books talk about hard earned wisdom. This one shows what that really looks like. The most impressive thing about Aaron isn't that he's been the first to realize many of the biggest trends in technology, it's how generously he has always shared his knowledge. If you're seeking a new way to think about your own usefulness in a rapidly automating world, Wired for Purpose is an essential read."

— Rohit Bhargava 3-time WSJ bestselling author and founder of The Non-Obvious Company

"Wired for Purpose is a sharp, human-centered blueprint for leading in an age defined by volatile, exponential technology. Aaron brings a rare combination of digital fluency, integrity, and in-the-trenches wisdom. He understands the internet's arc—where we've been and where we're headed—and grounds it all in service, curiosity, and connection. This is the kind of book that actually moves the conversation forward."

— John Battelle, author, entrepreneur, and co-founder, Wired

"You probably learned about the "4 P's" in your foundational marketing class. In "Wired for Purpose," Aaron Strout brings us the "3 H's," which forge a purposeful True North for moving forward: Humility, requiring us to check our ego before rushing headlong into the next shiny new thing; Humanity, keeping people at our center and not as props; and, Hope, which Aaron calls, "strategy's oxygen." Taken together, the 3 H's are our forcing function for doubling-down on our whole selves to progress, with hard head and open heart, to make our world better."

— Jane Sarasohn-Kahn, Health Economist, Advisor, Trend Weaver, THINK-Health and the Health Populi blog

"Wired for Purpose reveals how intellectual generosity becomes a force multiplier -- expanding your network, deepening trust, and driving meaningful results. The most enduring leaders lead with generosity. In this book, Aaron Strout offers a practical roadmap for building influence by lifting others."

When you help shape conversations, amplify emerging voices and create space for meaningful dialogue, your own voice rises with greater clarity and authority -- and your network strengthens with purpose. Wired for Purpose is both philosophy and playbook: a timeless guide for leaders ready to build or improve influence that truly matters."

— Bob Pearson, 4X Author, Teacher, Advisor and Investor

ACKNOWLEDGEMENTS

Writing a book is a solitary endeavor that is only made possible by a massive support system, and *Wired for Purpose* is no exception.

To my wife, **Melanie**: you are my ultimate north star. Thank you for your endless patience during this long process and for believing in this vision even when it was just a kernel of an idea. To my **kids Olivia, Benjamin and Audrey**: you are my constant reminders of why "purpose" matters in the first place. Your love and curiosity keep me grounded and inspired every single day.

To my **parents, Ron and Martha (I know you are tracking from up above)**: thank you for laying the foundation. You taught me the value of hard work and the importance of finding one's path. To my **brother John, and sister Heather**: thank you for being my first friends and my lifelong sounding boards. Our shared history is woven into the pages of my life and this book. Also a shout out to my in-laws, and my amazing nieces and nephews – I love you all so much.

I also want to extend my deepest gratitude to the professional communities and mentors who shaped my thinking. To Barb and Vin at **Bombaci + Mitchell** for giving me my start, to people like Lisa, Meryl and Sean at **Fidelity Investments** for taking a chance on me, to Barry at **Mzinga** for teaching me the power of thought leadership, Kathy, Joseph, Kursten and Natanya at **Powered**, and in particular, Jim, Bob, Paulo and Jenn at **Real Chemistry** for allowing me to build something special with you. Each of these organizations provided the "laboratory" where the ideas in this book were tested, refined, and brought to life. Your commitment to innovation and excellence set the standard for my own work. And a special shout out to my mentor and coach, **Milo**, who showed me the way in life and in work. You changed my life in a way that few others have. Also thank you to those that were kind enough to take time out of your busy schedules to be interviewed for this book and those that provided endorsements for the front cover.

Finally, to my **dearest friends like Erik, Joe, Gregg, Chris H., the boys of Gronk, my UMass boys from 55 Justice Drive, the Lafayette Peeps and too many others that I know I should mention**: thank you for the laughs, the love and the unwavering support. I am deeply grateful to have you in my corner. This book belongs to all of you as much as it does to me.

FOREWORD

When Aaron Strout invited me to write this foreword, I immediately accepted. Having worked together for more than a decade, I've seen him in action over the course of many iterations of the company I founded, Real Chemistry.

Throughout his career with me, Aaron showed incredible flexibility, dexterity and resilience through many periods of rapid change and growth. He was our Mayor of SXSW and CES, acting as the consummate Sherpa and emcee to clients, colleagues and friends alike.

His book, "WIRED FOR PURPOSE," is a blueprint for future leaders, offering honest insights into major business transformations driven by such things as M&A, technology adoption and world events, and practical advice on growth, burnout and career shifts.

Aaron highlights the importance of building your brand and fostering a valuable legacy and shares essential resources that have shaped the insight that drove his career. Aaron's straight-shooting advice on building a reputation and network is invaluable, particularly for those who understand the importance of their role within their community.

He directly addresses young professionals, providing actionable guidance to embrace perpetual learning and development to make a memorable mark on your communities, no matter your career path.

More than a collection of lessons, this book is a toolkit and a roadmap for meaningful success in a rapidly evolving landscape, most recently driven by the proliferation of generative AI.

Aaron's professional and personal reflections demonstrate his commitment to impactful, purpose-driven work. Dive in and be inspired to be the best you can be in your life and career.

Jim Weiss,
Founder and Chairman, Real Chemistry

PREFACE

When people ask why Aaron leads with generosity, why he pays things forward, remembers names, writes the thank-yous, my answer is simple: this is not a tactic; it's who he is.

Some of it is how he was raised. His parents were lovely, grounded people, and he learned early that if you treat everyone with equal respect, execs, admins, the person checking badges at the door, life moves with less friction.

He'll laugh about "relationship capital," but really he's just curious and considerate, long before he needs anything. When something does go off the rails, he isn't "calling in a favor." He's calling a friend. That's different.

I picture his career like a 400-foot ladder leaning against a wall. From the outside, people see him pop his head over the wall and assume he just appeared there. What they don't see are the thousands of rungs, early mornings, late nights, coffees with strangers, notes remembered, promises kept.

Back when everyone was playing with Foursquare, a neighbor once asked how Aaron suddenly had all these followers. I thought, you're seeing a few check-ins at the Starbucks; I'm seeing a decade of quiet climbing.

Analog Roots, Digital Reach

We're both Gen X, one foot in rotary phones and one in AI. That gives Aaron a kind of dual fluency, a love of real, human connection and an ease with the tools that extend it. When the world went home in 2020, what we missed most wasn't bandwidth; it was being in rooms together.

I think that's why his work resonates now: he's been "doing social" since before it had a name, not as a performance but as a habit of showing up, at conferences, on podcasts, in neighborhoods.

Optimism with Edges

We both believe you tend to receive what you project. But that only works if the kindness is real. Aaron's optimism is genuine and practiced. He loves encouragement, and for years, he struggled to metabolize hard feedback. Then he started working with Milo, who gave him a mantra we use at home: **feedback is a gift.**

That changed his posture at work and in marriage. He learned timing, tone, and how to hear the thing I'm actually saying, not just the words I'm using. We figured out the rule that the right conversation at the wrong time is the wrong conversation. It made us better.

He talks to our kids about arguments the way a debate coach would: *understand the other side so well you could argue it yourself.* That discipline, curiosity before certainty, lets him sit with people he disagrees with and find common ground. It's not performative; it's how he thinks. In a reactive world, that kind of rational optimism, breathe, state the facts, choose the next step, keeps the room from melting down.

Presence is Learned at Home

Aaron's dad traveled a lot for work but was present when he was home. Family first. That modeled something Aaron carries now. He can run hot professionally and still switch into full presence with us.

He has a strange, steady energy, less frenetic, more *okay, what's next?* Trim the tomatoes, fix the ceiling, help with homework. We also have a line we love when people ask who "wears the pants." We each have a leg. It's our shorthand for mutual respect: two adults, one rhythm.

People sometimes frame his career as luck or timing. I see the invisible practices. He remembers the admin's name, and her kid's soccer position. He checks in when there's no ask. He keeps conversations going between the crises so that when a real emergency arrives, the connection is warm, not opportunistic. You can call that networking if you want; I call it being a grown-up who pays attention.

What's Next

This book, his podcast, the speaking he does, this has been his goal for a long time, not as a victory lap but as a platform for service.

He'll never be the golf-every-day guy, but I do think he's building a life where we can travel more, say yes to the rooms that matter, and still get home in time to fend off a new colony of ants! (ha)

The work will evolve. The through-line won't: **show up, be kind, keep your promises, learn out loud, and make room for other people to shine.**

If you're reading his book to find the trick, here it is: <u>there isn't one. Just a 400-foot ladder and a man who keeps climbing it, one honest rung at a time.</u>

Lastly, let me share this… Aaron is a truly loyal supporter of those around him, he seamlessly smooths the edges of things otherwise uncomfortable and gracefully brings people together in a way that puts everyone at ease.

Aaron is a quiet "architect" of connection, as you'll see in the pages that follow.

Enjoy the read! - Melanie Strout

Introduction

I didn't set out to write a book about me. I set out to write a field manual about ***you***; how you build a career and a company that compounds, even as the tools and trends keep changing.

The title, **Wired for Purpose:** ***Why HUMANITY is the BIGGEST DIFFERENTIATOR in a DIGITAL WORLD,*** is deliberate. I've lived at those crossroads for three decades: pre-internet and proud of it, early to digital when it was a gamble, podcasting before the boom, and leading teams through social, mobile, and now AI. This book distills what those cycles taught me about people, progress, and possibility and how to practice leadership that lasts.

If you're a builder…operator, marketer, product leader, clinician-innovator, or founder…here's my promise: this is not a memoir dressed up as advice. It's a *user's guide* with stories. Each chapter opens with a scene you can feel and closes with concrete moves you can use…emails to send, experiments to run, rituals to keep.

The goal is pragmatic courage: do the next right thing, in the right spirit, at the right tempo.

So what qualifies me to write it? In short: I've done the work in public, across eras, and I kept the receipts. I learned to code when "view source" was the classroom. I led digital at scale inside a Fortune 100. I built podcasts into relationship machines long before they were fashionable. I helped grow a healthcare communications firm from roughly $47 million to a multibillion-dollar valuation, through calm leadership, disciplined experiments, and a relentless "thank-you first" culture.

Along the way, I made my share of mistakes: seasons where ego outran judgment and the best move was to own it, re-center, and rebuild trust. Those stories are in here, too, because durability is built as much by repair as by wins. This is a biggie!

This introduction is your map: what you'll get from each part of the book, why it matters now, and how to use it.

When we started tossing around book titles…*Analog Intelligence*, *Wired for Humanity*, *Wired for Purpose*, I kept coming back to the same conviction: I don't want a book *about* AI; I want a book about people.

AI will be with us for a long time, but my edge has always been the bridge…analog to digital, the connector's craft, and a thank-you culture I've actually lived. *Wired for Purpose* keeps the focus where it belongs. Humanity fuels it. Technology is the tool, not the headline.

What You'll Get (and Why It Matters)

The opening section establishes the frame. Purpose is the through-line; technology is the tool. The introduction you're reading sets the long-game mindset…why legacy matters, what I intend this book to do for you, and why I call it a "love letter" to the future of healthcare, tech, and leadership.

The thesis is simple: the next decade will reward leaders who can translate across tribes (scientists, technologists, operators, storytellers), hold a steady center under pressure, and practice gratitude as a system, not a mood.

Benefits you'll feel right away:

- A calmer decision rhythm, separating analysis from anxiety.
- A clearer filter for new tools…curiosity without hype.
- Practical rituals that increase trust, speed, and follow-through.

Chapter 1: Pre-Internet and Proud of It: Why Analog Roots Make Better Digital Leaders

Before dashboards and feeds, there were punch cards, dial-up, and the discipline of making things with your hands. My early years built a technical spine and a feel for people: how to learn, how to say thank you, how to make the complex simple.

This chapter shows how analog constraints sharpen judgment and why "life before infinite undo" is an advantage in an era of easy. You'll see how tactile beginnings translate into better product instincts, clearer communication, and more patient team leadership.

Use it to: audit your foundation…habits, standards, and the ways you learn…and restore a few of the constraints that make quality inevitable.

Going even farther back, way before cloud dashboards and social graphs, there were *punch cards*. My dad brought them home in the late '60s as scrap paper. I remember doodling on the backs of those cards, not knowing I was literally drawing on the language of machines. That kitchen table made me bilingual, tactile and technical.

It trained me to bet early on the right kinds of change: get curious, try it, learn fast, iterate. That posture has guided every chapter of my career.

Chapter 2: When Digital Was a Gamble: Betting Early, Learning Fast

In the 1990s, building websites, email programs, and banner ads wasn't cool; it was suspect. We designed intranets before most people knew the word and argued for attribution when the infrastructure didn't exist.

This chapter translates those first-principles into today's landscape: how to be early without being reckless, how to measure honestly when signals are messy, and how to earn trust when the organization isn't sure the internet (or AI) is "here to stay."

Use it to: run low-risk pilots with real success criteria, and put your new bets on the same scoreboard as the old ones.

Chapter 3: The Podcast That Preceded the Boom: Conversation as a Strategy

I launched my first show before iPhones existed. It wasn't about downloads; it was about doors; an excuse to have generous, focused conversations with people I respected. The medium gave me permission to build credibility by *featuring others*, and it taught me the hard discipline of listening back, killing filler, and responding to what guests actually said. You'll learn how to turn a podcast (or any platform) into a relationship engine that compounds.

Use it to: design a platform that serves guests first, creates teachable assets for your team, and seeds partnerships you can't buy with ads. (On my current show, ***Reaching Higher,*** I approach innovation through a human lens, drawing out heart, humor, and hard-won lessons from leaders across healthcare, tech, and transformation. That "human side of innovation" isn't branding, it's the method. https://reachinghigherpod.com/

Chapter 4: The Connector's Code: Networking as a Service

Most "networking" centers on the self. Mine centers service. The code is simple: make introductions you wish someone had made for you; show your work in public; keep score in gratitude, not favors owed.

This chapter shares stories of people I connected who later built companies, changed industries, or simply found their fit. More importantly, it breaks down how to operationalize connection inside your company so momentum isn't personality-dependent.

Use it to: create a weekly "NaAS" cadence; three value-forward touches, one thoughtful ask and to build an internal coalition that pulls with you.

Chapter 5: The Gratitude Engine: Thank-You as Operating System

Gratitude isn't a vibe; it's a system. Send the note, tag the win, credit the invisible work. Neuroscience and common sense agree: people who feel seen show up better. This chapter shows how "thank-you first" improved culture, sped execution, and made hard conversations easier. I'll share the everyday rituals that reinforced the habit and how gratitude became a durable source of advantage.

Use it to: install recurring calendar blocks, a public-credit routine, and a personal scorecard that tracks *who you lifted this week*.

Chapter 6: Rational Optimism in a Reactive World: Calm Beats Chaos

High-stakes leadership rewards calm, non-emotional thinking. Emotional neutrality isn't disconnection; it's direction. In this chapter, I walk through moments where staying level…slowing the "game" the way an elite quarterback does…protected teams, clients, and outcomes. You'll get tools to separate signal from noise, choose "Option C" when the world shouts A or B, and keep progress moving without pretending risk doesn't exist.

Use it to: practice in small stakes…breath + facts + next step…and build a reflex you can count on when the heat rises.

Chapter 7: Growing the Giant: How We Scaled (and What It Took)

This is the inside story of helping to grow a marketing agency from tens of millions to billions; what we got right, where we nearly lost the plot, and why shining the light on others became the growth engine. You'll see the inflection points that matter in any scaling arc: choosing unorthodox bets, building platforms that outlive people, and balancing ambition with integrity. The chapter is equal parts playbook and cautionary tale.

Use it to: name your next three scale levers and the guardrails that keep them healthy.

Chapter 8: The First to Try: Betting on Tools Without Drinking the Kool-Aid

After three decades of technology adoption, I've built a filter: curiosity + courage + ethics. This chapter shows how I vet new tools (AI included), what I predicted right (and wrong), and how to keep experiments small while designing for real proof, not hype. Think of it as a "build with" manual rather than a "wowed by" diary.

Use it to: define two-week pilots with a one-sentence success metric and decide *before* you start how you'll keep or kill them.

Chapter 9: Designing a Future That Heals: Tech x Marketing x Medicine

My day job and my obsessions collide here. I care about a world where technology lowers cost, increases speed, reduces invasiveness, and raises equity…*with humans in the loop*. We'll talk about work around glioblastoma and other frontiers where marketing, product, and clinical leadership must synthesize across tribes.

You'll see why marketers (the good ones) belong at the table: our best work is not "spin," it's *synthesis*; making the useful obvious, the complex usable, and the ethical non-negotiable.

Use it to: lead with questions a patient can feel and a clinician can use and to push for interoperability so insights flow where care happens.

Chapter 10: Legacy as a Leadership Principle: The Long View

Legacy isn't marble; it's daily practice. This chapter argues that the best leaders orient to the long term in a short-term world. Service over spotlight. Ownership over ego. You'll see letters I'd write to a younger me, and likely a note to your future self, too because what you rehearse now is the story you'll be living later.

Use it to: set a cadence you can live with when the spotlight is off and choose what you want "future you" to thank you for.

Why I'm the One to Guide You Through This

I'm a connector with a bias for service. On my shows, culminating in ***Reaching Higher***, I try to bring out "the human side of innovation." The through-line isn't celebrity; it's sincerity and usefulness. My career zigged across roles like Director of Digital Marketing at Fidelity and Chief Marketing Officer at Real Chemistry, where I stayed curious from the early days of social to the current rise of AI…always returning to the same question: how can tools help us serve real human needs? That's how I like to work behind the mic or behind the scenes…warmth, wit, and a knack for making complex ideas relatable.

I also did the unglamorous reps. I listened back to my own interviews and winced at the filler, "Love that," "Thanks for sharing"…then rebuilt the habit of actually responding to what my guest said. That discipline improved my interviewing, my leadership meetings, and my family dinners. Deep listening is transferable like that.

I learned humility the hard way. At times, I let recognition get ahead of contribution. Coming off a book launch and a run of keynotes, I arrived at a new company too full of my own story. The turnaround began when I stopped centering myself and started systematically featuring others…clients, colleagues, the quiet pros in the back row. That shift didn't just feel right; it worked. It was the formula we used to "get to the end zone," scaling an agency that people once underestimated.

I practice rational optimism…not cheerleading, but a disciplined refusal to catastrophize. When a marquee account wobbled and seven figures were at risk, I sat with our CEO and CFO, laid out the facts, modeled scenarios, and protected the team while we collected what was fair. Calm is a skill you can train, like a diver slowing their heart rate before a deep descent. That muscle has saved more projects than charisma ever could.

I believe in Option C. When the world offers a false binary, I look for the synthesis, often a smaller pilot with bigger upside, a candid conversation before a resignation, or a reframed brief that neutralizes the original constraint. This book will help you see "the third path" faster and make it real sooner.

I'm fluent in cross-tribe translation. I'm not the deepest scientist or the most hard-core engineer and I'm fine with that. My gift is synthesis: thesis, then antithesis, then synthesis. I listen widely, connect dots, and put complex ideas in explainable terms. In a moment when healthcare, AI, and experience design need each other, the translator's craft is not nice-to-have; it's essential.

And I'm still that kid who writes thank-you notes to executive assistants who guard the busiest calendars, to junior teammates who just shipped their first hard thing, to the mentor who told me a truth I didn't want to hear. Gratitude turned out to be the lowest-cost, highest-return investment I've ever made, and I intend to keep compounding it.

How to Use This Book

You can read *Wired for Purpose* straight through or "à la carte." If you're in a sprint and need steadiness, jump to Rational Optimism in a Reactive World. If you're building brand momentum without big budgets, start with The Podcast That Preceded the Boom and The Connector's Code. If you're navigating AI and healthcare, Designing a Future That Heals will give you a translator's toolkit you can use on Monday. The appendix is your on-ramp to deeper practice…books, tools, and frameworks that pair well with each chapter's exercises.

Each chapter ends with a Connector's Practice: three tiny moves: one ask to make, one thank-you to send, and one two-week experiment to run. The experiments are small on purpose. Cadence beats heroics. Publish the short post. Invite the guest. Try the tool. Then listen back, learn, and iterate.

If you lead a team, consider adopting the rituals out loud. Block 15 minutes weekly for gratitude. Build a running list of "Option C" decisions and what they unlocked. Hold a monthly "Always in Beta" retro: what we tried, what we learned, what we'll keep or kill.

The goal is not perfection; it's momentum with integrity.

What You'll Walk Away With

1. **A steadier internal climate.** You'll have words and moves for staying calm when stakes are high…breath, facts, next step…and the confidence that comes from reps, not pep talks.

2. **A relationship engine that scales.** You'll know how to turn platforms into trust, thank-yous into tailwinds, and generosity into real access, inside and outside your company.

3. **A practical filter for new tech.** You'll leave with a repeatable way to evaluate tools (AI included), run small pilots, measure honestly, and say "yes" or "no" without drama.

4. **A leadership stance that travels.** Whether you work in healthcare, software, consumer, or the public square, you'll have a method for convening smart people, translating across tribes, and building features that *heal*...in products, processes, and communities.

5. **A long-game lens.** You'll orient to legacy as a daily practice...service over spotlight...and design your weeks so the important things actually happen.

Not a memoir...a field manual with stories.

I'm not trying to write a hero's journey. I'm writing a user's guide. The timeline gives the book a spine, but every chapter ends with a move you can make: *one ask to send, one thank-you to deliver, one experiment to run.* My stories are there to make the patterns vivid and to prove these are skills, not gifts.

At 57 today, I grew up between analog and digital (born in '68)...doodling on my dad's punch cards and watching him dial into remote databases on a 9.6-baud modem by the fireplace. My mother's family hosted a Norwegian exchange student, Inger, in the '60s; at four years old I flew to Norway. Early exposure to other cultures widened my aperture and lowered my fear of new things.

Later, I chose Russian studies because I sensed a window opening with Gorbachev. That's my recipe for visionary thinking: broaden your lens on purpose, study history for analogs, and practice small leaps so bigger ones don't paralyze you.

Ego & Humility

Look, I've had seasons where my ego outran my judgment. At Fidelity, I was flying high after brokering meetings with leaders at Yahoo, eBay, and Costco, and nearly got bounced for believing my own press.

Years later, at the predecessor to Real Chemistry, I arrived hot off a book launch and social notoriety. I made the classic error of centering myself instead of clients and the brilliant healthcare voices around me.

The turnaround was simple and hard: feature others, build platforms, and measure myself by how well the team performed. That shift, plus relentless iteration, helped our firm grow from ~$100M to a multibillion-dollar valuation.

And yes, I discuss *all* of the details, the ugly, the bad and…the good…in this book.

The Coach who Changed my Operating System

The deepest rewire came through executive coaching with James Milosevic ("Milo"), starting around 2013–14 and continuing for years through retreats and one-on-one work.

He helped me separate confidence from ego, pursue *high performance without self-centering*, and institutionalize "always in beta." One of my favorite borrowed lines from Jim Weiss was, "If you think you've arrived, it's time to go." Coaching made that more than a slogan; it became muscle memory.

I still see Milo. The work keeps paying compounding interest.

Why Now

We are, once again, at a "hinge" moment. The same patterns I watched from analog to digital, from social to mobile, are playing out with AI and bio. The noise is loud. The stakes are high. The temptation to react is constant.

But the opportunity to lower cost, increase access, design for equity, and bring more humanity to how we build has never been bigger. The leaders who will thrive aren't the loudest or the most certain; they're the ones who can hold their center, synthesize across disciplines, and keep people first while shipping real outcomes. That's the work I love. It's the work I'm inviting you to do with me.

On Reaching Higher, I call myself "a natural connector with a gift for bringing out the human side of innovation." Whether behind a mic or shaping a brand's story, I try to make complex ideas feel relatable and keep us honest about the question that matters: *How can our platforms...podcasts, strategies, tools...bring more authenticity, empathy, and understanding into the world?*

If this introduction resonates, the rest of the book will feel like a long, candid conversation between colleagues who care about the same thing.

So take a breath. Pick your starting line. Send the thank-you. Make the ask. Run the tiny pilot. When you practice these moves week after week, purpose stops being a slogan and becomes an operating system. That's when careers get interesting, teams get brave, and companies grow in ways that improve real people's days.

It's still day one. Let's get to work.

CHAPTER 1: PRE-INTERNET AND PROUD OF IT

How the Early Years Shaped Everything to Come

It seems like a whole other world looking back now. 1993. Things were *really* different.

Before the web, business ran on paper, phones, and people. You found vendors and prospects in trade directories and the Yellow Pages, not Google. Research meant libraries, microfiche, and calling experts. Contracts moved by FedEx overnight or a bike courier across town; urgent revisions came through the fax machine, warm and curly.

And when it came to meetings, they were booked by your assistant over a landline, confirmed with calendar invites on paper (think Franklin Planners), and held in rooms with overhead projectors and acetate transparencies or a Kodak slide carousel if you were fancy.

Travel was arranged by a human travel agent. If you were out of the office, you checked voicemail from a pay phone with a calling card, returned pages from your beeper, and left word with reception.

Relationships were maintained through lunches, trade shows, and hand-written thank-you notes because there was no "quick ping."

Computers in 1993 were workhorses, not portals. Most offices ran MS-DOS or Windows 3.1 on beige desktops with 486 processors, 4–8MB of RAM, and chunky CRT monitors. Software lived on floppy disks; files were shuttled by "sneaker-net" (physically walking disks to a colleague) unless your company had a Novell NetWare server.

Spreadsheets were Lotus 1-2-3 or early Excel; documents were WordPerfect or Word; presentations meant Harvard Graphics or the first versions of PowerPoint, printed to transparencies on a laser printer.

Email existed on closed systems like cc: Mail or Lotus Notes, but many teams didn't have it yet; memos were paper, and routing slips were literal. Modems chirped at 2400–14.4 kbps, used mostly for dial-up bulletin boards or remote access, not for "browsing," which almost no one did.

Mobile phones were rare, heavy, and expensive; most business was conducted from a desk phone, a conference room speakerphone, or the trunk-mounted "car phone." And somehow, deals still closed because coordination, trust, and follow-through were muscles everyone used every day.

Yep…it was the early 1990s, and "going online" wasn't something you did casually while waiting for your coffee.

It was an ordeal. It was an event. And more often than not, it didn't work the first time.

We didn't "Google" things. We asked people. Actual people. We didn't have YouTube to walk us through a fix. We had three-ring binders, dog-eared manuals, and if we were lucky, a mentor who didn't mind explaining the same thing three different ways until it stuck. And if you lost that manual? You weren't just out of luck, you were in the wild.

The 1990s: Dial-Up, Yahoo and the Code Before Google

Even though I had a passion for computers and technology in the early '90s, I was never truly an IT person. I joked that I was the de facto IT guy at my previous college/grad school jobs since I knew how technology worked. And I did learn to code in Basic and played Dungeons and Dragons online (all words, no graphics) back in the early to mid-80's, but that was something I did on my own for fun.

Dial-up internet was the "soundtrack" of the late 20th century. That modem handshake, half screech, half static, was like listening to two robots try to whistle at each other from across a canyon. You'd connect, wait, pray, and hope no one in the house picked up the phone and ruined your shot at downloading that one text file you'd been waiting 25 minutes for.

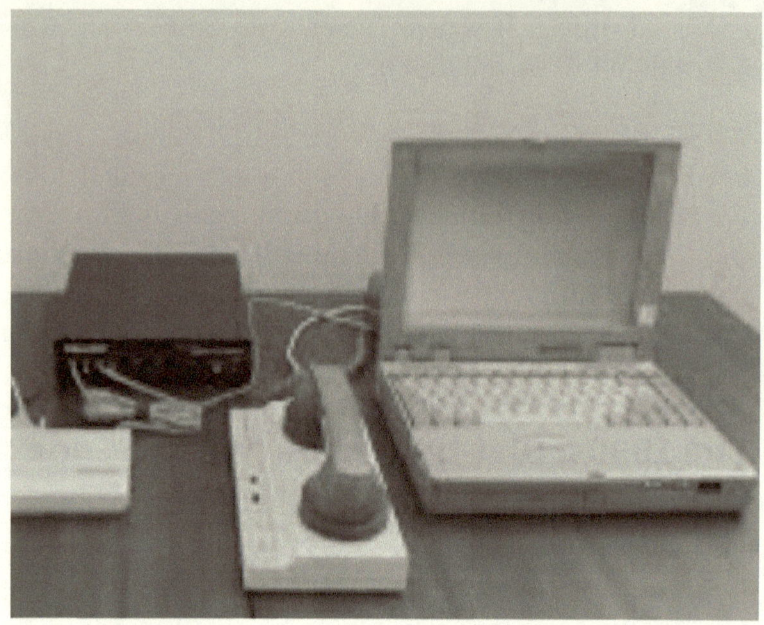

YAHOO!®

There was no such thing as a quick answer. If you were debugging, you were *really* debugging. If you were researching, you weren't typing in keywords, you were flipping through indexes and calling someone you thought might know. Every solution you found was hard-won, and because of that, it stuck with you.

That's one of the gifts of the pre-internet era: nothing came instantly, so everything felt earned.

And Google was not even an idea yet. Yahoo came along first. Yahoo was the web's front door, a human-edited directory turned all-in-one portal where millions began their online sessions to browse categories, check news, finance, and sports, and use free Yahoo Mail.

It bundled basic search with curated links, bustling chat rooms, early instant messaging (Yahoo Pager), and personalized "My Yahoo" homepages, creating a daily dashboard for mainstream users. In that pre-Google moment, Yahoo's homepage was one of the most-visited destinations on the internet. Yeah, like I mentioned, things were really different back then.

How I stumbled into marketing while the web was being born

I finished a contract as a database architect and got a curveball: the VP of Marketing I'd worked for said her parents' direct-marketing shop needed an account lead and someone who could "help with the email and the Internet."

There wasn't Wi-Fi. There was barely a web. They offered to train me in the basics of copy, list hygiene, and direct mail if I could figure out websites and Photoshop. So in 1994, I taught myself HTML with no WYSIWYG editors, mocked up a fold-out-brochure style site, and discovered the first big lesson that's guided my whole career: learn the fundamentals, then translate them to the new medium. A friend told me the Internet was a fad. We still laugh about that.

Banner ads, email, and "Is this ROI real?"

I joined Fidelity in 1997 and we started running some of the company's first banner ads…1–3% click-throughs in the Wild West before IAB standards. We also pushed hard into email. The hard part wasn't ideas; it was attribution. We could count impressions and clicks, but closing the loop to "did this open an account?" took years of tagging, landing-page discipline, and culture change.

We fought the same battle everyone fought: a banner ad rarely causes a complex financial action by itself, so we had to educate leaders on multi-touch journeys and build media-mix models that put digital on the same scoreboard as mail, TV, and radio.

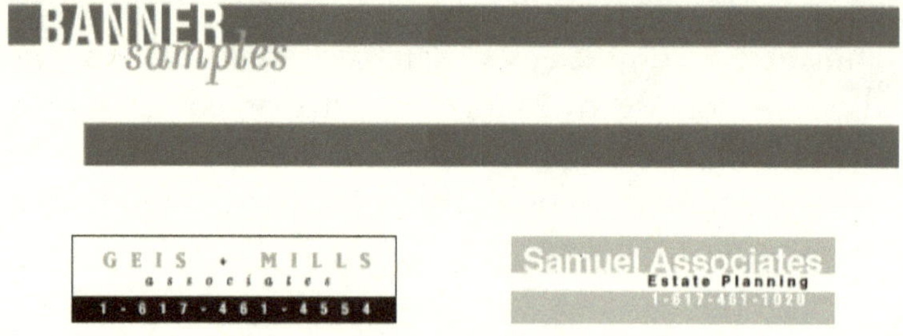

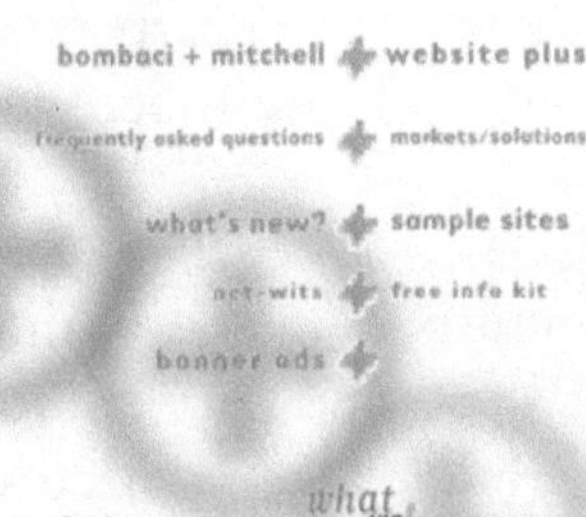

How far ahead I tend to see (and where I don't)

In the mid-90s, I could imagine today's early-2000s web, richer media, brand interactivity, and better communication. By '07–'08, in the first wave of location-based marketing, I pictured walking into a store, virtually trying on clothes, and just…leaving, no cashier, no friction, your phone orchestrating the rest.

Some of that took a decade to show up. I rarely see 30 years out; I try to see one generation ahead and act on it. (That's why I left Fidelity in 2006 for a startup focused on online/offline community as social networks were emerging).

Building a Technical Foundation in a Pre-Digital World

Looking back, I realize those years weren't just "the way things were", they were training. They were sharpening the habits and the instincts that I would lean on decades later as a digital leader.

First, I learned to respect architecture. When breaking something meant days of work lost and sometimes thousands of dollars wasted, you didn't take shortcuts. You studied. You understood the dependencies. You tested before you committed.

Second, I learned patience. Waiting for a program to compile wasn't dead time; it was planning time. You mentally ran the next step. You rehearsed possible outcomes. You anticipated where the system might fail. That space for reflection is rare today, but back then it was built into the work.

Third, I learned resourcefulness. Without Google, your network was your lifeline. You'd call people who might have a clue, ask for their notes, barter for a copy of a script they'd already written. You didn't just "find answers," you earned them.

Fearless and teachable

If there's a through-line in my story, especially back in the wild, wild west 1990's, it's action without bravado. I come by it honestly. Way back in the 1950's, my grandmother served as a city clerk and then a state legislator when few women ran; my dad jumped into early computing and startups because the frontier called.

That pattern became my practice: study Russian before it was fashionable, lean into internet marketing before it was obvious, and embrace social/location-based tactics before most had language for them.

When Wiley asked me to write a For Dummies book, I didn't feel "ready." I said yes anyway and did the work. Here's the lesson I keep relearning: the worst most people will do is ignore you…more often, they say yes. Courage, it turns out, is a behavior you can train: make the ask, place the small bet, learn in public, repeat.

My grandmother, Barbara Strout

Analog → Digital → Outcomes

Before the Internet, I was not precious about tools. And I'm still not. I'm precise about *outcomes.* Push edits and prevention to the front of the process. Design experiences that reduce friction. Build habits that make relationships scale. In marketing terms: zig when everyone zags, place a few unorthodox bets, and measure the useful things…introductions made, doors opened, ideas shipped. In human terms: be generous, be specific, be consistent.

As I mentioned in the Introduction, I practice what I call *rational optimism*…not cheerleading, but a disciplined refusal to catastrophize. When trends get noisy, I separate analysis from anxiety. Decide, act, review, evolve.

That stance shapes how I network (ask with humility), how I lead (thank-you first), and how I learn (small experiments scaled by evidence). The result isn't endless positivity; it's durable momentum.

Why Understanding Analog Life Made Me a Better Digital Leader

When the internet finally became the constant backdrop of our lives, I saw something the younger techs didn't: they thought the digital world was permanent, infallible. They'd never had to do without it.

I'd seen systems fail for reasons no one could predict: power surges, humidity in the server room, a cleaner unplugging the wrong cable.

I understood that tools could vanish, that data could be lost, that redundancy was a mindset, not a feature.

That awareness made me cautious with shiny new tech. I didn't reject it, but I asked questions: What problem does it actually solve? How will it change the way we work? What happens when it breaks? Will it make us better, or just faster?

I knew, too, that relationships were more important than perfect systems. Some of the best solutions I'd ever seen came not from a manual, but from a conversation. Coffee and trust often solved more than code and upgrades.

Case Study: The Handwritten Contract

It was 1995, and email was still a novelty in most offices. If you wanted something in writing, you didn't fire off a PDF; you put pen to paper.

We'd just landed a potential new client, a small but fast-growing manufacturing outfit. The CEO, a guy in his early 40s who still wore grease-stained coveralls to meetings, was old-school. He believed in a handshake and a contract you could hold in your hands. The catch? He needed a finalized agreement in 24 hours or he'd go with another vendor.

The legal department was swamped. Our fax machine, our "fastest" means of delivery, was out of toner, and the nearest supply store had just closed for the night. The younger guys on the team shrugged, figuring there was nothing to be done until morning.

But I'd grown up in a world where you didn't wait for perfect conditions, you made do. I called the legal assistant at home, dictated the contract line by line over the phone while she wrote it out by hand, then drove across town to pick it up. By midnight, I was in my own kitchen with a pot of coffee, neatly typing the text into a word processor one painstaking paragraph at a time.

The next morning, I was at the CEO's plant at 8:00 a.m., the contract in a manila folder under my arm. He signed on the spot.

That deal turned into a five-year relationship worth six figures. But what stuck with me wasn't the number; it was the reminder that tools change, but commitment doesn't. When you decide something matters, you find a way.

Analog Thinking in a Digital Age

What those early years gave me, more than skills, more than technical knowledge, was **a way of thinking.** ***Analog thinking.***

Analog thinking values the process as much as the outcome. It respects the limits of tools and works within them creatively. It assumes that things will break, and plans for that breakage. It recognizes that human connection is the real network behind any system.

In the years that followed, as digital tools became faster, sleeker, and seemingly foolproof, I never lost those instincts. They've been my anchor in high-stakes moments, my compass in a world that moves too fast for its own good.

Closing Reflection: Why It Still Matters

Here's the thing about coming of age in a pre-Internet world: it makes you immune to the myth that speed is everything.

Back then, speed was *relative*. A fax was "instant," a FedEx overnight was a miracle, and waiting three minutes for a file to load wasn't a crisis, it was just part of the process. That pace gave you room to think, to anticipate, to prepare for what might go wrong before you charged ahead.

Those habits have kept me grounded in every leadership role I've ever taken. When a server goes down, I don't flinch. When a market shifts overnight, I don't panic. I've lived in systems where nothing was guaranteed, and I know that steadiness is more valuable than any piece of tech you can buy.

I'm not nostalgic for dial-up or paper jams or my Yahoo home page. I'm grateful for what they taught me: that resilience isn't built in moments of convenience, but in moments when you have to make something work with what you've got. That the best tools in the world can't replace patience, persistence, and human connection. And that, no matter how fast the future comes at you, the principles you carry from the past are the ones that will keep you steady.

The truth is, analog life didn't hold me back; it set me free. It taught me to see the long game, to value the people as much as the process, and to never mistake the latest tool for the right tool.

And in a world obsessed with what's next, that might just be the most important advantage of all.

CHAPTER 2: WHEN DIGITAL WAS A GAMBLE

What it meant to be an early adopter when everyone else waited

It's hard to explain to someone who grew up with Wi-Fi in their back pocket what it felt like to open a web browser in 1996.

Not the sleek, minimalist interfaces we have now, but a clunky gray box that took 45 seconds to load a single page, if you were lucky.

Images arrived pixel by pixel, top to bottom, in a slow reveal that felt less like technology and more like waiting for a Polaroid to develop. And the whole time, you were listening to the faint electrical hum of your computer tower, hoping no one picked up the phone and kicked you offline.

Back then, "going digital" wasn't a foregone conclusion. It was a risk. The kind of gamble that had the power to make you look like a visionary or a fool, depending on how the chips fell.

Most companies in the mid-'90s didn't have websites, email was barely creeping into daily business use, and online advertising was… well, let's just say we were making it up as we went along.

For me, those early years weren't about catching a trend…they were about chasing a possibility. The possibility that this clunky, unrefined technology would someday be as essential as a phone line or electricity.

And the only way to prove it was to start building before anyone else believed.

Designing the First Websites

In 1996, when I was at the direct marketing agency, Bombaci + Mitchell, the first website I ever worked on looked nothing like what we think of today.

Forget mobile-friendly. Forget CMS platforms or drag-and-drop design. Forget even "easy" HTML.

We were coding by hand in text editors, manually setting table widths to align images, and praying the client wouldn't change their logo after we'd painstakingly sliced it into GIFs.

A mid-sized insurance client came to us with one question: *"Why would we need a website?"*

It was the question of the era, and it came in many variations:

- "Our customers already know us."
- "The Internet is for kids."
- "We don't sell anything online, so why bother?"

To them, a website wasn't a necessity. It was an expensive brochure that nobody had asked for. But we saw it differently. We saw it as a 24/7 handshake…a way to be visible in a place that, one day, everyone would visit.

That first site was six pages. Home. About. Products. Services. Contact. And one page we convinced them to add called "News," which we updated every few months by literally rewriting the HTML file. There was no CMS, no WordPress, not even Blogger. Just raw code, an FTP login, and the thrill of seeing your work appear on a screen halfway across the world.

When the site launched, they were underwhelmed. "This is it?" they asked. "This," we said, "is the front door to the future."

Email Campaigns When Spam Didn't Exist (Yet)

If websites were a tough sell, email campaigns were even harder. Most business owners in 1996 didn't have email addresses. The ones who did treated their inbox like a private mailbox, only checking it once a week. Marketing by email sounded, to them, like telemarketing by fax machine.

We had one retail client willing to take the plunge. Their "email list" was literally a typed-out Word document with about 85 addresses, collected at checkout over several months. We built an email template from scratch; no HTML email editors, no marketing automation, just a clean block of text with their logo pasted in as an inline image. When we sent that first campaign, half the recipients replied asking, *"What is this? How did you send me a letter through my computer?"*

But a few days later, the client called:

"We had people come in mentioning the email. They bought things. This works."

That was the turning point for me. Not because we'd "invented" anything, but because I saw how quickly skepticism could turn into trust when you showed results.

Banner Ads Before There Were Rules

Today, online ads follow you around like persistent salespeople. In 1996, they were just starting to appear.

Banner ads were 468 pixels wide, 60 pixels tall, and lived at the top of a page like digital billboards. They were static images linked to a website, and the industry-wide click-through rate was around 44%, not because they were brilliant, but because people had never seen them before.

We designed one for a local law firm. It featured a single JPEG image of the client's logo and their phone number. The client thought it was too simple.

But when the ad went live on a local news site, it drove more calls in two weeks than their print ads had all year. They doubled their online ad spend the next month.

It's almost comical now, the ad was a grainy photo with a clickable rectangle, but it worked because the playing field was wide open. There were no algorithms to fight, no saturated feeds to compete with. Just you, your idea, and a handful of people who dared to believe the web was worth showing up for.

The Skeptic in the Corner Office

One of the clearest memories I have from those early days in 1996-97 happened in a paneled boardroom that smelled faintly of cigar smoke and old carpet. The CEO, a man in his late sixties, proud of his decades in the print advertising world, sat across from me with his arms crossed.

"Son," he said, leaning forward just enough to make me aware that my tie was crooked, "I've been selling products longer than you've been alive. People like to hold what they buy. They like to look someone in the eye before they spend money. The Internet? That's just… noise."

It would have been easier to back down. To nod politely, shake his hand, and leave with my pitch folder still closed. But something in me knew this was exactly the moment early adopters lived for, the opportunity to convince a disbeliever not with hype, but with possibility.

So I asked him a question: *"Do you think your grandchildren will still read the newspaper?"*

He laughed. "Of course not. They're too busy with their Game Boys."

"Exactly," I said. "And the people who figure out how to reach them now will be the ones they buy from later."

He didn't sign that day. But he called a month later after hearing his competitors were "messing around online" and told me to "build him one of those websites." He never admitted I was right, but he became a client for years.

Selling to People Who Couldn't See the Web

One of the stranger challenges of the mid-'90s was selling websites to people who literally couldn't see them. Many executives didn't have Internet access on their work computers. Some didn't even own a home computer.

We'd bring what can be roughly equivalent to a laptop to meetings, fire up a modem, and hope we could get a stable connection before they lost interest. Sometimes it took so long to load a single page that we had to narrate what they would see if the images appeared.

It was like selling a car to someone by describing how the engine sounds without ever letting them drive it. You relied on storytelling, on painting a vivid picture of the possibilities. And if you were convincing enough, they'd nod slowly and say, "Alright. Let's try it."

The Day the Gamble Paid Off

There was no single moment when everyone suddenly "got it." But there were turning points, small victories that stacked until the risk felt less like a gamble and more like inevitability.

One of those moments came when a longtime skeptic, a wholesale distributor who had refused a website for years, called me out of the blue. "My competitor's website," he said, "is showing up before us in search results. We need one now. Yesterday."

We built it in record time. And when orders started coming in through the site within weeks, he called again, this time with a different tone. "I don't know why I waited so long. This thing's like having another sales rep who never sleeps."

Helping others cross the fear line

You know, not everyone is wired to post, ask, or experiment publicly. I've coached friends through first comments on LinkedIn, first outreach, first pilots. The ROI of one action is tiny; the ROI of cadence is massive.

When Mike Schneider and I wrote *Location-Based Marketing for Dummies*, we packed it with <$100 experiments because small wins are the on-ramp to momentum. The principle still holds for generative AI: define a safe, tight experiment; name success in a sentence; run it for two weeks; keep or kill without drama.

Making Everything Easier!™

Location-Based Marketing FOR DUMMIES®

Learn to:

- Choose the right location-based service to achieve your goals
- Get started using foursquare®, Facebook Places, Yelp®, and Gowalla®
- Analyze the results of your program
- Apply and adapt what other businesses have learned

Aaron Strout
Mike Schneider

Ego, humility, and almost getting fired...*twice*

Back in the day, I had quite a few moments where my ego outran my judgment. At Fidelity, I was flying high after brokering meetings with leaders at Yahoo, eBay, and Google and nearly got bounced for believing my own press.

Years later, at the predecessor to Real Chemistry, I arrived hot off a book launch and social notoriety. I made the classic error of centering myself instead of clients and the brilliant healthcare voices around me.

The turnaround was simple and hard: feature others, build platforms, and measure myself by how well the team performed. That shift...plus relentless iteration...helped our firm grow from ~$50M to a multibillion-dollar valuation. (more on that later)

Closing Scene: The First Big Win Email

It was late, maybe 9:30 p.m. in our cramped office above a downtown coffee shop. A single desk lamp threw light across the keyboard. We were running updates on a client's site when the office email pinged.

The subject line read: Order Confirmation.

We stared at it for a second before opening it. It was an online purchase for a $249 item from a customer three states away. The timestamp showed 9:14 p.m….well after the store had closed.

We didn't cheer. We didn't high-five. We just sat there for a moment, letting the reality sink in. The thing we'd been trying to explain for months had just proven itself without a single word.

That was the moment we knew. The gamble was over. The future had arrived.

CHAPTER 3: THE PODCAST THAT PRECEDED THE BOOM

Two Decades of Voice, Curiosity, and Community

The first episode of The We Show wasn't recorded in a soundproof studio. It wasn't even recorded with a proper mic. It was cobbled together on a desk in the corner of my office, a nest of tangled wires and a chunky laptop that wheezed every time it processed an audio file.

This was 2006, before the iPhone, right after YouTube started, before "podcast" had a dictionary entry.

If you wanted to distribute audio online, you weren't uploading to Spotify or Apple Podcasts; you were wrestling with FTP clients, XML feeds, and RSS tags that had to be hand-coded. Every episode was a small battle in a war against both bandwidth limitations and cultural skepticism. People still looked at you funny when you told them they could "subscribe" to an audio program on the internet.

That first episode was me interviewing the chairperson of our company's Business Process Management (BPM) conference about some of the highlights. Pretty boring stuff, right? But our CEO was bullish on using some of these new Web 2.0 tools, like blogs and podcasts, to promote our traditional events.

We eventually decided to call the podcast *The We Show* because when I joined Shared Insights as CMO, they had a book project called "We are Smarter than Me". It was in the vein of "Wisdom of Crowds" by James Surowiecki. The book focused on people and companies that were using online community to improve their products and platforms. So I started to interview leaders from the companies as well as other online community experts.

And I'll be honest, those early episodes were rough. You could hear my chair creak. Guests sometimes sounded like they were phoning in from the bottom of a well. Editing was me, hunched over headphones at 1 a.m., splicing out awkward pauses in Audacity and praying the file wouldn't corrupt on export.

But here's the thing: every episode taught me something about people. About curiosity. About the kind of leadership that comes from listening more than you speak.

The Gamble No One Asked Me to Take

In 2006, starting a podcast wasn't an entrepreneurial "move." It wasn't a growth hack. It was a hobby for tech nerds and audio experimenters. I wasn't chasing ad dollars or sponsors, I was chasing a conversation I didn't see happening anywhere else.

The gamble wasn't just technological; it was reputational. There was no playbook for how a podcast could help a business or build a brand. If anything, people assumed it was a distraction from "real work."

I remember telling a colleague I was thinking about launching *The We Show*. He blinked at me, tilted his head, and asked, "So… like a radio show on the internet? Who's going to listen to that?"

Fair question. The audience for podcasts in 2006 was microscopic compared to now. But I didn't care. I had a gut sense that long-form conversation would be the antidote to the shrinking attention spans I was seeing everywhere else in marketing. Banner ads and email blasts were fighting for fractions of seconds. A podcast could hold someone's attention for 30 minutes, or longer, if you earned it.

That was the gamble. Not just that someone would listen, but that someone would listen long enough to matter.

Why I started podcasting and what I was really doing

The show gave me something more valuable than downloads: permission to build relationships with people whose names could lift an unknown brand.

I learned quickly that a podcast invite opened doors others couldn't: most guests said yes because the medium felt novel, and those intimate conversations created real ties.

That pattern: borrow credibility, create value for the guest, earn trust…became a through-line I've used ever since.

By the way, my comfort on the mic didn't come from nowhere. In high school, I did two musicals, *Brigadoon and Fiddler* on the Roof and I discovered how much work it takes to carry a live stage. Around 21, a friend and I shot spoof videos on a clunky camcorder and held family screenings. I had no idea I was practicing for the digital age; I only knew I liked making things and wasn't afraid of an audience.

That blend of art and tech is why digital fit me: I could teach myself HTML and Photoshop, assemble assets, and ship.

FIDDLER ON THE ROOF

Director .... Mr. Joseph D. Messina
Orchestral Conductor .... Mr. Burt Ross
Choreographer .... Mrs. Judith Clark
of the Judith Clark Academy of Dance
Assistant to the Choreographer .... Allison Lynch
Speech and Interpretation Consultant .... Dr. Kenneth Crannell
Emerson College
Lighting Design .... Kenneth Matteucci
Rehearsal Pianist .... Mrs. Mary Fabrizio

CAST OF CHARACTERS

Tevye, the Dairyman .... Keith Woods
Golde, his Wife .... Marla Cerulli
Tzeitel (his Daughters) .... Frances Donovan
Hodel (his Daughters) .... Helena Oliveira
Chava (his Daughters) .... Andrea Pecci
Shprintze (his Daughters) .... Melody Stout
Bilke (his Daughters) .... Kim Montgomery
Yente, the Matchmaker .... Eugenica Vagianos
Motel, the Tailor .... Mark Ballard
Perchik, the Student .... Christopher Hornbarger
Lazar Wolf, the Butcher .... Ben Smith
Mordcha, the Innkeeper .... Mike Grogan
The Rabbi .... John Murphy
Mendel, his Son .... James Regan
Avrahm, the Bookseller .... John Garofalo
Yussel, the Hatmaker .... Mr. Arthur Poulos
Nacham, the Beggar .... Donald Felker
Grandma Tzeitel .... Christine Williams
Fruma-Sarah .... Lisa LeBlanc
The Constable .... Aaron Strout
Fyedka .... David Sullivan
Shaindel, Motel's Mother .... Kristen Bates

and

The Fiddler .... Christopher Grogan
Villagers .... John Adams, Cheryl Aloi, Chris Dugan, Marcy Grogan, Cindy Jachrimo, Michelle Koehler, Lisa LeBlanc, Allison Lynch, Kim MacPherson, Karen Mullaney, Pamela Muse, Lori Nelson, Terry Ryan, Kim Short, Christine Williams
Russian Dancers - Bottle Dancers .... Darren Clark, Tim O'Regan, David Sullivan
Chavaleh "dream sequence" Dancers .... Allison Lynch, Cheryl Aloi, Lori Nelson
Village Boys .... Christopher Mills, Athanasius Vagianos

Generalist bones, specialist muscles

As I've mentioned, I grew up bilingual (analog and digital). I've always been a strong generalist: decent at math, science, and English without needing to be a purist in any one lane. Curiosity is the multiplier. It pushed me to explore early social/location marketing, and to keep "jumping curves" as new maturity cycles began. I rarely see 30 years out; I try to see one curve ahead and act on it.

The long arc of the mic

I've essentially been podcasting nonstop: *WE Show* (2006–2008), *Quick & Dirty* ('08–'11), a video podcast series *Live from Stubb's* ('12–'15), then *What2Know/Real Chemistry* through early 2025, and now *Reaching Higher* (launched June 2025). The medium dipped for a while and then *Serial* (2014) pulled it back into the mainstream, but by then the habit was baked into how I build. Thousands of hours later, the ROI stacks up in three layers:

- **Personal:** a master's-level education in interviewing, storytelling, and deep listening.
- **Company:** a top-ten growth lever that helped us punch above our weight, book A-list speakers, and warm relationships.
- **Network:** trust that leads to referrals and key opinion leader introductions you can't buy with ads.

LIVE FROM
AUSTIN, TEXAS
STUBBS

What podcasting taught me about listening

I forced myself to listen back to every episode. Brutal. I heard the filler, "Love that," "Thanks for sharing", and realized I was sometimes marching to my next question instead of honoring the answer in front of me. I rebuilt the habit: check the next prompt quickly, return full attention to the guest, respond to what they actually said, and let silence do its job. That's when conversations got real.

Networking as a Service (NaaS)

I treat connecting like software: always on, embedded everywhere, and designed around the other person's "what's in it for me." Before a conference, I research who will be in the room and what matters to them. I lead with assets that help them…an invite to the podcast, a spot on a panel, a warm intro…not an ask to buy something.

That approach routinely lands "out-of-my-league" guests and senior leaders because the value is clear, the tone is respectful, and the follow-through is consistent.

Reading the room in a polarized world

People joke that I'm "The Senator" because I try to see both sides without losing my own center. I've hosted civil threads on hot topics by setting rules up front: respect or you're out. When I opened a discussion on Facebook after yet another school shooting, hundreds of comments later, we had a useful exchange…hunters, activists, doctors…because I enforced tone, not ideology.

That practice shows up offline too: understand the driver beneath someone's position, acknowledge it, and then make your case. It's empathy with a spine.

Case Study #1: The Skeptical Guest

One of my earliest guests was the vice president of corporate communications at Netflix back when they were still mailing DVDs out to customers vs. streaming. They were quickly replacing BlockBuster as the leading distributor of box office movies and getting someone of his stature was a big deal for me. But he almost didn't come on the show.

"Look, Aaron," he said over the phone, "I'm not sure what this is. I don't want to waste my time if only twelve people are listening."

I told him I couldn't promise numbers, but I could promise depth. "It won't be a soundbite interview. We'll go deep, and you'll have the space to explain things people don't get yet."

He agreed, reluctantly.

Midway through the episode, something shifted. His voice loosened. He told a story about Netflix's decision to stream movies to PCs, which at the time was a huge bet for them. It was raw, personal, and nothing like the rehearsed answers I'd heard him give on stage.

After the episode aired, he called me. "I've had more thoughtful emails about this podcast than about my last three keynote speeches combined," he said.

That's when I knew: podcasting could make people *feel seen* in ways no other medium could.

Why Conversation Builds Credibility Faster Than Content

It's one thing to post a thought leadership article. It's another to invite someone into an unhurried conversation where you're not trying to "win" or "close" anything.

Conversations reveal the connective tissue of ideas, how someone thinks, not just what they think. They slow the pace down enough for trust to form. In a podcast, credibility isn't asserted; it's *earned in real time.*

In the early to mid 2000s, marketing was obsessed with "content is king." I was starting to realize that content without conversation was just noise. People didn't just want more information; they wanted a reason to believe the person giving it to them.

Podcasting gave me a front-row seat to that truth.

Case Study #2: The Episode That Escaped Its Audience

We recorded an episode with Janna Anderson, a professor at Elon University and director of their "Imagining the Internet" project. I assumed it would be a niche listen, a handful of fellow Elon students and professors and maybe some internet nerds.

Two weeks later, my inbox was full of emails from other professors and even a state senator's office. Someone had posted the episode to a national education forum, and it spread like wildfire.

That episode did more to raise awareness for his cause than months of PR. And it wasn't because the production quality was flawless (it wasn't). It was because the conversation was real. She wasn't pitching, she was sharing. And that authenticity traveled further than any marketing plan we could have made.

What Podcasting Taught Me About Listening

When you sit across from someone, whether physically or virtually, and your only job is to hear them, you start noticing things you miss in everyday conversation.

The pauses. The way someone inhales before they answer a hard question. The shift in tone when they start telling a story they *really* care about.

Podcasting trained me to listen for what wasn't being said. And in leadership, that's gold. Because the decisions that matter most often hinge on the unspoken, the hesitation in a team member's voice, the silent agreement in a room when no one wants to break the ice.

Case Study #3: The Interview That Changed Me

One guest, named Amberly Lago, now a best-selling book author and motivational speaker who'd survived a near-fatal accident that led to a dangerous addiction to alcohol, taught me more about resilience in one hour than I'd learned in a decade of business.

She spoke about failure with a kind of peace that was disarming. She was in a constant state of pain, but her unbridled optimism really struck me.

That interview has stuck with me ever since. And I wouldn't have heard it if I'd been filling the space with my own voice instead of making room for hers.

The Community We Didn't Know We Were Building

By late 2007, *The We Show* had listeners in over a dozen countries. Not millions, but enough to create a community that felt tight-knit, almost secret. People would email me saying they'd been listening to every single show.

Some guests became clients. Some listeners became collaborators. Some episodes sparked entirely new ventures I couldn't have planned for if I tried.

Looking back, I realize the podcast wasn't just a platform. It was a practice. A ritual of curiosity and connection that shaped not just my business, but my worldview.

The Evolution of the Podcast

By the early 2010s, the world had caught up to the idea of on-demand audio. Smartphones put podcasts in every pocket. Platforms like iTunes and later Spotify normalized the idea that you could listen to niche conversations whenever you wanted. Suddenly, the thing I'd been explaining for years didn't need explaining anymore.

But with that shift came a new challenge: noise.

In 2006, the problem was convincing people that a podcast was worth their time. By 2015, the problem was standing out in a sea of new shows, all with sharp branding, polished intros, and marketing budgets I couldn't have imagined in the early days.

Case Study #4: The "No PR Script" Rule

About six months in, I started noticing a pattern. Some guests would show up with polished talking points, phrases I'd heard them repeat in other interviews word for word.

So I instituted a rule: *No PR scripts allowed.* Guests could bring bullet points, but I reserved the right to throw them out the window if the conversation went somewhere better.

One CEO came in ready to talk about a new product launch. Ten minutes in, I asked him about the biggest professional risk he'd ever taken that didn't pay off. He froze. Then he laughed. "No one's ever asked me that."

For the next twenty minutes, he told the story of a failed expansion into Europe, the lessons it taught his team, and how it forced him to rethink leadership. When the episode aired, the feedback was overwhelming, not about the product launch, but about his candor. People related to him because he'd let them see the cracks in the armor.

That's when I knew my role wasn't to be a platform for press releases. It was to be a space where honesty outranked marketing.

Why Long-Form Still Wins in a Short-Form World

As TikTok, Instagram Reels, and Twitter soundbites became the currency of online attention, I kept hearing the same advice: "Shorter is better. People don't have time."

And yet… our longest episodes back in the day often had the highest engagement.

Here's why: long-form conversation creates *immersion.* Once someone invests in the first five minutes, they're far more likely to stay for the next fifty if they're learning something, laughing, or feeling connected.

Short-form media can make you aware of an idea. Long-form lets you *inhabit* it.

The Unplanned Education

Looking back now, my third show, the *What2Know Podcast* (we rebranded it to be the *Real Chemistry Podcast* when W2O Group became Real Chemistry) became my unofficial MBA in people. Our CEO, Jim Weiss, who wrote the foreword to this book, sat me down one day and said, "Why don't you start another podcast – one focused on clients and other industry experts?" In less than a month, we had the new pod up and running and recorded some of our first episodes at Wired Magazine co-founder, John Battelle's NewCo Festival. My very first episode of the new show was with celebrity chef, Tyler Florence. It was pretty epic.

During this show, I learned how to read between the lines. How to sense when a guest is holding something back and how to earn the trust to bring it forward. How to listen for patterns, not just in what was said, but in the stories people chose to tell.

The show didn't just give me content; it gave me insight. And insight is the currency of leadership.

Case Study #5: When the Mic Became a Mirror

There was one guest, Jason Calacanis, who was a digital pioneer and early investor in web-based companies, who came in radiating confidence. We talked about scaling, hiring, and the future of investing. Midway through, I asked a simple question: "What keeps you up at night?"

He hesitated. The room went still. Then, almost sheepishly, he admitted he didn't know if he was the right person to lead the company at its next stage.

That vulnerability changed the tone instantly. Listeners later told me it made them think about their own self-doubt differently, that if someone that successful could question himself, maybe it was okay for them to, too.

The mic can be a megaphone. But sometimes, it's a mirror.

Case Study #6: The Call from an Old Listener

Last year, I got a call from someone I'd never met. He introduced himself as the head of analytics at a Fortune 50 company. "You don't know me," he said, "but I listened to your podcast in 2007. I wanted you to know that an episode you did with Angie Hicks, founder of Angie's List (now just Angie), changed how I built my team. We've been working together for ten years now because of that conversation."

It's humbling when you realize something you made in a tiny, makeshift studio almost twenty years ago can still shape someone's career today.

What Podcasting Gave Me That Nothing Else Could

It gave me patience in a world that rewards speed. It gave me depth in a culture that often stays shallow. It gave me a way to serve without selling.

And maybe most importantly, it gave me a reason to keep asking questions, even when I thought I already knew the answers.

The Practice That Never Gets Old

Now with my brand new podcast (more on that later), I still get a little nervous before hitting "record". Not because I'm afraid of what will happen, but because I know what *could* happen. One conversation can change a mind. One story can reframe an entire industry.

That's the thing about podcasts, you never know which moment will land, which line will stick, which story will travel. But you keep showing up, mic on, ears open. Because somewhere out there, the right person is listening at the right time.

Closing: The Long Echo of a Single Conversation

It's funny how the sound of a mic clicking on can feel the same after twenty years. The equipment has changed. The platforms have evolved. But the ritual remains: Deep breath. Adjust the levels. Glance at my notes, then shove them aside. Lean in. Listen.

When I think about that first recording back in 2006, the one in a room barely bigger than a closet, with gear that would make today's podcasters laugh, I remember the uncertainty. Not about the conversation, but about the point of it all. Would anyone care? Would anyone listen?

Now I know the answer: someone always cares, and someone is always listening. And you rarely know who, or when, or how your words will find them.

The two-year experiment that was *The We Show* proved something I carry into every room I lead, every team I build, every strategy I shape: voice builds bridges faster than content ever will. A blog post might inform. A tweet might provoke. But a conversation, unedited, unscripted, and human, creates a bond.

And here's the thing: the bonds outlast the broadcast. The interview ends, but the connection lives on, in follow-up calls, in collaborations, in quiet moments when a listener replays something you said because it matters to them right then.

Leadership works the same way. Your title might fade. Your projects might wrap. But the way you made people feel, the clarity you offered when the noise was loud, the humanity you brought when the stakes were high, that sticks.

I sometimes wonder if the real value of *The We Show* wasn't the show itself, but the mindset it trained into me. The patience to let a story unfold. The discipline to listen without rushing to reply. The courage to ask one more question when silence hangs in the air.

It's a strange thing, to look back over thousands of hours of conversation and realize they were never just interviews. They were leadership lessons in disguise, about trust, about presence, about the long game of building something that matters.

The world today moves even faster than it did in 2006. Attention is shorter, tempers are quicker, and noise is louder. But the core hasn't changed: people still crave connection. They still want to be seen, heard, and understood.

And that's the through-line I'll never let go of. Whether it's a podcast mic or a boardroom table, the job is the same: make the space, set the tone, and trust the conversation to do its work.

So here's my quiet advice to anyone thinking about starting something, whether it's a podcast, a business, or a movement: **start.**

…Even if you don't know who will listen. Even if you're years ahead of the curve. Even if the world thinks it's a gamble.

Because twenty years from now, you might find that what you began in a closet with a borrowed mic became the thing that taught you how to lead.

And you might just discover that the real purpose of the work wasn't the platform you built, but the person you became while building it.

CHAPTER 4: THE CONNECTOR'S CODE

I've never liked the word "networking."

It sounds transactional, like there's a ledger somewhere keeping score, how many cards you handed out, how many names you collected, how many favors you banked.

That's not how I've ever approached it. To me, the real magic isn't in stacking up contacts, it's in building bridges you may never personally walk across. Sometimes you introduce two people and disappear from the frame.

Sometimes those two people go on to build something extraordinary together, something that changes industries, launches movements, or sparks friendships that outlast any market cycle. And you don't need your name etched in the foundation stone to feel the weight of that legacy.

In the early days, when I was still learning the rhythms of leadership and the strange currency of influence, I noticed that the most remarkable people I met didn't actually spend much time talking about themselves. They spent their time asking questions, drawing threads between ideas, and noticing who in the room might be better off knowing each other.

I started doing the same…not as a tactic, but because it felt good. It felt human. Somewhere along the line, it became what people expected from me: that I'd know who they should meet next, even if they couldn't articulate why they needed to meet them yet.

One Tuesday afternoon years ago, I sat in a half-empty coffee shop with a woman whose startup was barely holding on. She was smart, driven, and stuck. Her technology was solid, but she couldn't get a foothold with the right customers.

Two days earlier, I'd had lunch with a quiet, meticulous founder in a completely different industry who was about to face a challenge she didn't yet see coming. Something in my gut told me these two should meet. They were from different worlds, but their instincts and ethics aligned. I sent an email that took all of forty seconds to write.

Six months later, their companies had entered into a partnership that not only saved one from collapsing but catapulted the other into a market leadership position. My name never appeared in their press release. I didn't want it to. That wasn't the point.

The point was that a bridge existed where before there had been a gap.

When you treat connecting as an act of service instead of self-promotion, something shifts in the way people respond to you. They let down their guard. They remember you not as the guy pushing a business card into their palm, but as the person who genuinely cared about where they were going and how they might get there faster, better, with less collateral damage. I've had people call me ten years after an introduction to say,

"That conversation changed everything for me." And it's not because I'm some wizard who sees the future, it's because I listen for the threads. I listen to what's said, what's unsaid, and the story in between.

In one particularly telling moment, I found myself at a crowded conference reception. Two attendees stood on opposite ends of the room, each orbiting their own small circle. One was a brilliant young engineer who'd just built a prototype for a healthcare device. The other was an established executive with deep manufacturing contacts overseas.

Neither had any idea the other existed, even though they were both scanning the room for "opportunities." I walked over, tapped each on the shoulder, and said, "You two need to talk." I stepped back, let the current take over, and within minutes they were leaning in, sketching diagrams on cocktail napkins. They went on to co-develop a product that got FDA clearance and is now saving lives. My role? I just drew the first line on the map. They built the road.

This is what I've come to think of as **The Connector's Code:** See the person, not the title. Hear the potential, not just the pitch. Make the introduction with no strings attached. And then step out of the way.

It's not glamorous. In fact, sometimes it means you won't get credit for the seed you planted. But if you're wired for legacy instead of applause, you start to understand that the real return on investment is the world that gets built because you nudged two paths to intersect. That's enough. That's more than enough.

Over time, the people you've served in this way start to do it for others. They carry it forward without being asked, without keeping score. That's when you know it's not just something you do…it's a culture you've created.

And in a culture like that, trust becomes the most valuable currency in the room. Deals move faster, conversations go deeper, and relationships outlast transactions. You stop being just another name in someone's CRM and start being the person they think of when they hear, "Who do you know that…"

I've been in rooms where billion-dollar deals were on the table, and I've been in rooms where someone just needed a friendly nudge to meet the person who would become their co-founder. In both cases, the principle is the same: you're not there to extract value, you're there to create it. And when you do that consistently, without needing to broadcast your role, you find yourself at the center of a network that's alive, dynamic, and self-sustaining.

Years from now, most people won't remember every product you launched, every campaign you led, or every metric you hit. But they will remember how you made them feel, who you helped them meet, and what doors you helped them open. That's the gift of the connector. And if you do it right, it's a gift that keeps moving long after you've left the room.

The Connector's Path (and why gratitude comes first)

Over the years, podcasting became my "laboratory". Week after week, I sat down with interesting people, asked real questions, and then did the unglamorous follow-through: send the note, make the introduction, say *thank you* publicly and privately.

Gratitude isn't a nicety; it's network infrastructure. It enriches the guest, cements the learning, and compacts future friction. Over time, the show turned into a super-connector engine. Ideas, partnerships, friendships: because I led with appreciation and showed up consistently.

Fearless and teachable

If there's a through-line in my story, it's action without bravado. I come by it honestly. My grandmother served as a city clerk and then a state legislator when few women ran; my dad jumped into early computing and startups because the frontier called.

That pattern became my practice: study Russian before it was fashionable, lean into internet marketing before it was obvious, and embrace social/location-based tactics before most had language for them.

When Wiley asked me to write a *For Dummies* book, I didn't feel "ready." I said yes anyway and did the work. Here's the lesson I keep relearning: the worst most people will do is ignore you…more often, they say yes. Courage, it turns out, is a behavior you can train: make the ask, place the small bet, learn in public, repeat.

But all of the above has really come from my passion for connecting others. Because many of them have paid it back to me and those have turned into new opportunities.

Honestly, though, I was never looking for that. It just *happens.*

Not every connection turns into a blockbuster success story

That's something worth saying out loud, because the point of this work isn't to bat a thousand, it's to keep showing up to the plate. Some introductions fizzle. The timing isn't right. The chemistry's off. Life intervenes.

But even in those misses, something invisible is happening people are learning to associate you with possibility. They're learning that if your name shows up in their inbox or your number flashes on their phone, what follows is likely to be an open door. That reputation, over time, becomes its own form of leadership.

One winter morning, I found myself on a layover in Chicago, killing time in an empty gate area. A young marketing manager from a mid-sized tech firm recognized me from a talk I'd given months earlier and came over to say hello. We got into a conversation about her company's struggle to break into a heavily regulated market. Her voice carried that mix of determination and exhaustion I've heard countless times in leaders trying to drag an idea uphill. I asked a few questions, jotted down a couple of notes, and when I got home later that night, I sent an email introducing her to a compliance consultant I trusted completely.

They ended up working together for years. I never saw a dime from that connection, but months later she told me that single email shaved eighteen months off their go-to-market timeline. Sometimes the value you add doesn't show up on your own balance sheet; it shows up on someone else's, and that's fine. In fact, it's the whole point.

The second case study lives in an entirely different industry. Years ago, a friend in the entertainment business was lamenting over dinner about the talent pipeline drying up for a specific kind of production work. "We just can't find people who can do it right," he said, shaking his head. I thought back to a conversation I'd had weeks earlier with a small-town college professor whose graduating students were desperate for a way into the industry but had no contacts, no internships, no ladder to climb.

One phone call later, I had them on a group Zoom. The professor set up a portfolio showcase for the students, my friend's team attended, and within weeks, three graduates had full-time jobs. None of those students knew my friend existed, and my friend didn't know where to find them. All it took was a bridge, and the willingness to build it without worrying about who'd get the credit.

These moments don't just happen because you have a big Rolodex. They happen because you're listening, cataloging, and remembering; mentally bookmarking potential intersections that may not occur for weeks, months, or years. The Connector's Code isn't about quick wins; it's about laying the groundwork for collisions that will matter later. If you can keep your ego out of it, you'll be surprised how fast people come to trust you with their most sensitive introductions.

And here's the other thing: it's not just the people at the top of the ladder you should be connecting with. One of the most destructive myths in "networking" culture is that your focus should always be up…toward the most powerful, most visible, most "valuable" people in the room. That's a scarcity mindset disguised as ambition.

The junior staffer you connect with today could be the decision-maker in five years. The intern could be your client. The overlooked could be the one who builds the product everyone else ends up using. Seeing people for where they could be, not just where they are, is one of the most underrated leadership skills there is.

It reminds me of a CEO I once knew who kept a single rule for introductions: she never introduced two people based solely on their current titles. She connected them based on character, potential, and values. "Titles change," she told me once over coffee. "Values don't." I've carried that with me ever since.

The best connectors operate like gardeners. They plant seeds without knowing exactly when, or if, they'll sprout. They water relationships over time. They don't yank on the stem to make the plant grow faster. They trust the process. And when the bloom finally comes, they stand back and admire it without needing to point out who put the seed in the ground.

Networking as a Service (NaAS)

I treat connecting like software: always on, embedded everywhere, and designed around the other person's "what's in it for me." Before a conference, I research who will be in the room and what matters to them.

I lead with assets that help them, an invite to the podcast, a spot on a panel, a warm intro, not an ask to buy something. That approach routinely lands "out-of-my-league" guests and senior leaders because the value is clear, the tone is respectful, and the follow-through is consistent.

That practice shows up offline too: understand the driver beneath someone's position, acknowledge it, and then make your case. It's empathy with a spine.

EQ is the Through-Line

I spent 14 years at Real Chemistry by reading the room, elevating others, and measuring myself by team outcomes. Coaching helped me separate confidence from ego and stay "always in beta."

The operating rule I still use: feature the guest, credit the team, and let the work speak. That's how you keep doors open and compounding.

Helping Others Cross the "Fear Line"

Not everyone is wired to post, ask, or experiment publicly. I've coached friends through first comments on LinkedIn, first outreach, and first pilots. The ROI of one action is tiny; the ROI of cadence is massive.

Boosting people up and giving them a litte feel good positive "juju" is part of the whole connecting thing. I always seek to make the connection a positive, proactive one in every way.

The Connector's Code in Action

A few years back, I was invited to speak at a private leadership event in San Francisco. About fifty executives were in the room, each with their own agendas, their own industries, their own set of challenges. After my talk, during the informal mingling, I spotted a quiet man in the corner, the CEO of a medical device company. He seemed content to just observe, but when I struck up a conversation, he told me about a problem his company was facing getting his device reimbursed by insurance companies was proving to be challenging.

Coincidentally, another attendee, the COO of a mid-sized insurance company and I were talking at lunch, and he let me know that his company was looking to shed the stereotype of traditional payers and truly help patients get access to the treatments and therapies they needed. I walked each across the room to the other.

Two years later, those two companies were working closely together to help patients with severe sleep apnea not only sleep better, but to do so without spending an arm and a leg. Every time I see their quarterly results in the news, I think back to that quiet moment in the corner of that San Francisco venue. That's the thing about the Connector's Code…you never know which introduction will change the arc of someone's story. You just keep making them.

The Connectors Code Field Guide

I've been asked more times than I can count, *"How do you know who to connect, and when?"* The answer isn't a formula; it's more like reading the weather. You watch the patterns, you feel the shifts, and you learn to trust your instincts.

Still, over the years, I've noticed certain principles that always hold true. I'm going to tell them to you the way I learned them through moments, not manuals.

1. **The Name You Almost Forgot**

   One Thursday afternoon, I ran into a guy whose name I almost couldn't place. We'd met briefly at a dinner six months earlier. Instead of ducking the moment, I leaned in. I asked him about a project he'd mentioned back then, and he blinked, surprised I remembered.

That conversation turned into a partnership between his firm and someone I introduced him to a week later.

Lesson: Memory is currency. People will remember that you remembered.

2. The Two Minute Email

After a panel I spoke on, a young founder caught me in the hallway. Her product was clever but lacked distribution. I knew a regional retailer who was hunting for exactly that category. That night, I sent a short email: "You two need to know each other." A month later, they had a contract.

Lesson: Never underestimate the two-minute introduction. Done often enough, it rewrites careers.

3. The Long Game

Years ago, I introduced two people at a conference. They chatted for a while, but nothing came of it…at least not then. Three years later, one called me to say they'd just closed a major deal together.

Lesson: Some seeds take seasons to grow. Plant them anyway.

4. The Sideways Bridge

It's tempting to only connect people "upward" toward power. But some of the most fruitful introductions are lateral…people at the same stage, with complementary skills. I once connected two mid-level managers who shared a vision for a new product. Today, they're co-founders.

Lesson: Never underestimate the peer connection.

5. **The Disappearing Act**

When you make an introduction, step back. Don't hover, don't referee, don't look for updates like a kid checking the oven. I've had introductions that blossomed precisely because I didn't insert myself into their momentum.

Lesson: Be the bridge, not the tollbooth.

6. **The Quiet Ask**

Every so often, someone will hint at needing help without saying it. A sentence, a sigh, a subtle pause. Those moments are gold for a connector, if you're listening. I've saved more opportunities from dying in silence simply by saying, "Tell me more about that."

Lesson: Listening is your superpower.

That's the Connector's Code. Not rules carved in stone, but habits worn into muscle memory. The more you practice them, the more natural they become, and the more people will start to see you as the person who sees them.

Connector's Code: Leadership Addendum

The same principles I use when connecting people outside the office work just as powerfully inside it. A leader who knows how to see connections others miss is a leader who can turn a good team into a great one.

When you remember a team member's idea from a meeting six months ago and circle back to it, you're doing the "Name You Almost Forgot" in leadership form. You're proving you were listening, not just hearing words. That's the kind of moment that makes people feel like their contributions matter, even if they didn't make the final cut at the time.

The "Two-Minute Email" becomes a two-minute note of recognition. When you quickly connect a teammate's small win to a company-wide goal and share it with others, you build momentum and trust at the same time.

The "Long Game" shows up when you back someone's potential before the rest of the company sees it. Promotions, stretch assignments, and mentorships are all bets on seeds that might not sprout right away, but when they do, they can reshape the whole organization.

"Sideways Bridges" are just as important in leadership. Too many managers only send talent upward toward executive exposure. The best leaders connect peers across teams, creating horizontal alliances that break down silos and accelerate problem-solving.

And the "Disappearing Act"? That's delegation. Trust your people to take ownership of an opportunity you've set in motion without hovering over every move. Your absence becomes a vote of confidence.

The quiet "Tell me more" moments…when you catch a hesitation in someone's voice and dig deeper…can save a project from derailing, or a good employee from leaving. It's leadership by listening, and it's rare.

In the end, leading with the Connector's Code is about making your team feel like the right connections, whether ideas, people, or opportunities, are always within reach. And when they feel that, they start creating their own connections too, multiplying your impact without you ever having to ask.

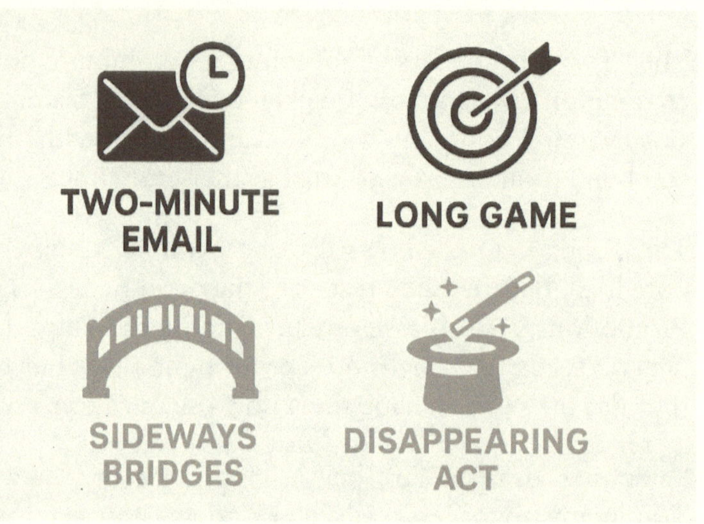

How gratitude became an operating system

I grew up in humble circumstances with parents who insisted on thank-you notes and noticing people. That training stuck. Early at Fidelity, I learned the power of being genuinely kind to executive assistants, remembering birthdays, saying hello in crowded rooms, treat them as partners.

Work gets easier when people feel seen. I built on that with small, consistent deposits: comment on someone's post with something specific, text a quick "thinking of you," send a 30-second birthday video instead of a generic "HBD."

Most people wait to reach out until they need something; I try to reach out when I don't. Over time, those touches compound into advocacy.

The Boomerang Moments

Gratitude comes back in surprising ways. Fifteen years after a quick career chat with a friend of a neighbor, she resurfaced as a tech VP and credited that conversation with giving her the confidence to leap. Another time, I went to bat for a former accounts-payable colleague, quiet, overlooked, out of work, by vouching to a CMO I barely knew; she landed the job.

And when a talented teammate, Meredith, left our firm, I told her sincerely, "I'm here if you ever want to come back." Eighteen months later, she did and became one of our most important leaders. None of that was a tactic. It was a practice.

Make people feel seen (on purpose).

I look for the unique thing about someone and name it publicly: the way they prepare, the clarity of their questions, the steady hand they bring when others spin out. Inside a company, that shows up as celebrating promotions, sending quick congrats, and amplifying quiet wins.

Externally, it's offering value before I ask: a podcast invite, a warm intro, a panel slot. Networking becomes a service, not a transaction.

Beautiful things can happen when you connect people!

CHAPTER 5: THE GRATITUDE ENGINE

The Secret Leadership Fuel Behind Everything

It never started as a strategy. Not at first.

I didn't wake up one morning and think, *I'm going to build a leadership philosophy around the word 'thank you."*

Like most things that end up shaping the arc of a career, it began as something smaller, almost invisible, until it wasn't. Until it became a lever I could pull in any boardroom, in any creative war room, in any late-night production deadline scramble, and watch the tension drain out of the air like someone had cracked open a window.

The earliest version of The Gratitude Engine came from a moment most people wouldn't have noticed. I was standing in the cramped kitchen of our first office, a space that always smelled faintly of burnt coffee grounds and the ghost of microwaved leftovers. One of our junior designers, quiet, sharp, and often overlooked, was rinsing out a stack of mugs after a long day. She wasn't on kitchen duty. She wasn't asked. She was just… doing it.

I remember pausing in the doorway, watching her, and thinking how easy it would be to keep walking. She wasn't looking for recognition. She was probably lost in thought, planning her evening. But I stopped, and I said it: *"Thank you."* Not the flat, reflexive version we all say at checkout counters, but the kind where you actually mean it. The kind where your voice changes just slightly, like you're telling someone they matter.

Her head lifted, eyes blinking as if to confirm I was talking to her. She smiled, a small, genuine curve, and said, "Sure." But something shifted. I saw it. She stood a little straighter.

That moment became my first data point. Over time, I started tracking these tiny "thank you" moments like a quiet scientist observing cause and effect. It didn't take long to notice the pattern: when people felt seen, they gave more. Not because they had to. Not because of the paycheck. But because they wanted to.

The Science Behind the Word

This isn't just sentimentality dressed up in leadership jargon. Neuroscience has receipts. Studies from the University of California, Davis show that practicing gratitude activates the brain's medial prefrontal cortex, the region linked to learning, decision-making, and emotional regulation. Gratitude literally rewires the brain to focus on positive outcomes, building resilience under stress.

In a workplace context, that's leadership gold. The Journal of Applied Psychology reports that leaders who express authentic appreciation see a measurable uptick in team performance and engagement. Gratitude boosts oxytocin, the "connection hormone", while reducing cortisol, the stress hormone that clouds judgment and erodes focus.

In other words, *thank you* isn't just polite. It's a neurological intervention.

When the Engine Kicks In

One of the first times I saw the Gratitude Engine operate at full power was during the crunch leading up to a product launch. The kind where deadlines are measured in hours, not days, and every department is running hot. I had a teammate named Allie, tough, exacting, built for high-pressure work.

We were in the war room, surrounded by empty coffee cups, stale air, and the rhythmic click of keyboards. Allie was managing three simultaneous crises: a vendor delay, a client who'd just decided on a major messaging shift, and a copywriter who had been awake for thirty hours straight.

I could have barked out, "We need this fixed now!" Instead, I walked over, stood next to her, and said quietly, "I see what you're doing. Thank you for holding this together. You're the reason this launch is going to happen."

It took less than five seconds to say. But I watched her shoulders loosen. I watched her inhale deeper. She smiled, not the forced smile of someone "managing up," but the kind that carries oxygen back into the soul. And then, without missing a beat, she went back to typing. Faster. More focused.

That's the thing about the Gratitude Engine: it doesn't just lift morale; it sharpens performance. People will sprint for a leader who notices their effort.

Making People Feel Seen

At its core, gratitude is about visibility. In a noisy workplace, where attention is a currency spent mostly on problems, it's easy for the human contributions to disappear under the weight of metrics, KPIs, and Slack notifications.

When you make someone feel seen, truly seen, you're giving them a piece of emotional equity in the outcome. It's the difference between "I did my job" and "I helped *build* this."

A Gallup survey found that employees who receive regular recognition are 31% more productive and 33% more likely to stay with their organization. But here's what the data doesn't capture: the subtle transformation in a person's eyes when they know they matter. That flash of "I belong here." You can't fake that. And once someone feels it, they will defend the culture that gave it to them.

Gratitude as Cultural Architecture

Some leaders treat culture like interior design, something you decorate a company with once the real work is done. But culture is not furniture; it's the architecture. And gratitude is the steel beam in that framework.

I learned this the hard way in a previous role, where the culture was driven by fear. Leaders hoarded praise like it was a finite resource. Wins were absorbed into the collective without individual acknowledgment, while mistakes were broadcast and punished.

The result? Turnover rates high enough to make the *HR* department feel like a revolving door. Burnout. Creativity in free fall.

When I finally took over my own team years later, I reversed the formula. Public gratitude became a default setting, not an annual award ceremony. If someone nailed a presentation, we said it *in the room.* If a developer quietly solved a bug no one else could crack, we thanked them *in front of the team.*

It wasn't just good manners; it was strategy. People who feel appreciated are more likely to go all-in when it counts. They're more likely to speak up with ideas, to take ownership, to push past "good enough." Gratitude, given freely and often, doesn't just make people feel better; it makes them *better performers.*

Everyday Rituals

The Gratitude Engine isn't powered by grand gestures; it runs on the small, repeatable rituals that accumulate over time. In our weekly team huddles, we closed with a quick "gratitude round." Each person named one colleague they wanted to thank and why. At first, it was awkward; people defaulted to safe, surface-level compliments. But over months, the answers deepened.

"Thanks to Jen for staying late last night to help me meet a deadline."

"Thanks to Missy for jumping in on client calls even when it wasn't her project."

It became a feedback loop. The more people expressed gratitude, the more they noticed things to be grateful for. The room changed. The *work* changed.

In leadership, you learn quickly that what you ritualize, you normalize. Gratitude became our default mode, our cultural gravity. And when crisis hit, as it inevitably does, it was gratitude that held us together.

Crisis as a Gratitude Stress Test

If you really want to know whether your Gratitude Engine is working, test it under pressure.

Our biggest trial came during an analytics dashboard rollout with a Fortune 50 client just before the Consumer Electronics Show (CES) in early January. We had been building toward this launch for months, every milestone hit, every roadblock cleared. Then, less than forty-eight hours before go-live, we realized there was a flaw in our code. Not just a small bug, an all-hands-on-deck, "this changes everything" flaw that threatened to sink the whole thing.

AARON
STROUT

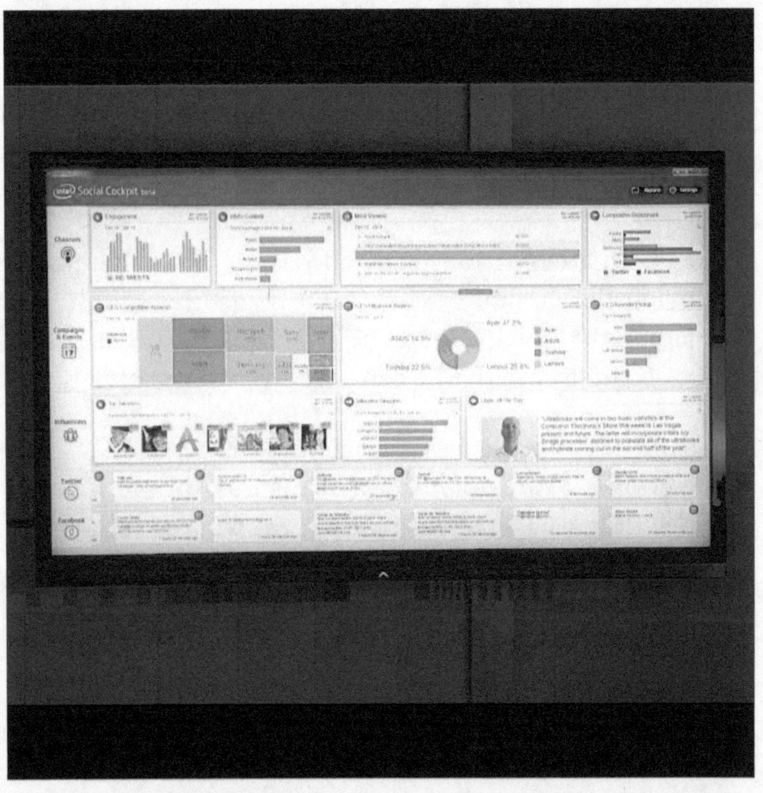
Social Cockpit

Gratitude in
Leadership

I walked into the project room that morning and saw a dozen faces lit by the glow of laptop screens, the air heavy with caffeine and adrenaline. This was the kind of problem where leaders are tempted to command and control, to bark orders and demand overtime.

Instead, I gathered the team and said, "First, thank you for being here. I know you could be at home with your families right now. You're here because you care. That means more to me than I can say. Now, let's solve this."

It wasn't a speech. It was a recalibration. Gratitude before instructions. Humanity before hustle. And it worked. People didn't just work hard; they worked smart. By midnight, the system was live.

Why It Works Under Fire

In neuroscience terms, gratitude interrupts the amygdala hijack, that stress-driven survival mode where we default to fight, flight, or freeze. When you thank someone, authentically and in the moment, you're engaging their prefrontal cortex, the part of the brain responsible for reasoning and problem-solving

Under high pressure, that shift is everything. It's the difference between a developer staring blankly at their screen and one who suddenly remembers a workaround from a previous project. It's the difference between a marketing lead shutting down or picking up the phone to call a favor in from a vendor.

The Gratitude Engine doesn't erase the problem; it primes the people to solve it.

Gratitude as Invisible Leadership Infrastructure

A lot of leadership is visible: the speeches, the strategy decks, the company-wide emails. Gratitude, by contrast, works like the building's HVAC system; most people won't notice it when it's functioning, but they'll feel the difference when it's gone.

When gratitude is absent, resentment starts to build like stale air. Misunderstandings multiply. People question whether their contributions matter. Slowly, productivity begins to suffocate.

But when gratitude is embedded in the infrastructure, when it hums quietly in meetings, emails, casual hallway exchanges, it becomes self-reinforcing. New hires pick it up within weeks. Senior leaders model it without being told. And when the air feels clean, people breathe easier and perform better.

The Cost of Neglecting It

I once consulted for a fast-scaling tech startup that was hemorrhaging talent. On paper, they were a dream: high salaries, stock options, glossy perks. But inside, there was a vacuum where gratitude should have been. Wins were transactional. Recognition was rare.

When I interviewed departing employees, a phrase kept surfacing: *"I just didn't feel appreciated."* That sentence is the quiet death knell of culture. They weren't leaving for more money; they were leaving for oxygen.

Replacing them cost the company hundreds of thousands of dollars in recruitment and training, not to mention the lost momentum from institutional knowledge walking out the door. A two-second "thank you" could have saved them millions.

Gratitude as a Competitive Advantage

It's worth noting that gratitude is not "soft" leadership. It's a performance multiplier. When Bain & Company studied what drives employee engagement, one of the top predictors of high performance was whether people felt recognized for their contributions. Recognition, they found, fuels discretionary effort, the kind you can't mandate in a job description.

Think about that: if two companies have the same talent, the same budget, and the same tools, the one that systematically thanks its people will win. Not because they work more hours, but because they work with more heart.

Gratitude isn't just morale. It's math.

Every day in the Field

I've made it a point to run my Gratitude Engine in places that seem least likely to need it, moments when things are going well.

A few years ago, we'd just wrapped a major conference. Weeks of planning, thousands of attendees, flawless execution. The team was exhausted but riding the high of a clean win. Most leaders would have celebrated the success and moved on to the next big thing.

I didn't. I pulled each person aside, every single one, and thanked them for a specific contribution. Not a blanket "thanks for your hard work," but targeted recognition: "That keynote ran so smoothly because you caught that slide deck error," or "The way you handled that last-minute speaker cancellation saved us."

You could see it in their eyes; they felt seen not just for the *outcome*, but for the *process*. Gratitude in moments of triumph is like investing in emotional savings for the next storm.

The Rituals That Keep the Engine Running

There are dozens of ways to hardwire gratitude into a company's DNA, but the most effective for me have been the ones that become rituals.

1. **Gratitude Rounds** – At the end of weekly meetings, each person thanks someone else for a specific action that week. Over time, it trains people to notice effort.

2. **Personalized Notes** – Handwritten cards, even for small wins, have a disproportionate impact. I've had team members keep them pinned to their desks for years.

3. **In-the-Moment Acknowledgment** – Never wait for a performance review to say thank you. The closer the recognition is to the act, the more it lands.

What's critical here is consistency. Gratitude isn't a marketing campaign; it's a muscle. The more you use it, the stronger it gets.

Gratitude and the Long Game

Over the years, I've realized that the Gratitude Engine has an almost compounding effect. The same junior designer I thanked in that office kitchen. She went on to become a senior leader herself, running her own team with gratitude at the center. I've watched dozens of others do the same.

Gratitude, it turns out, scales.

And maybe that's the secret leadership fuel behind everything: it's not about creating moments where you look good as a leader, it's about creating a culture where *everyone* looks for opportunities to make someone else feel essential.

When that happens, the work changes. The company changes. And you change with it.

CHAPTER 6: RATIONAL OPTIMISM IN A REACTIVE WORLD

Leading Without Panic, Pressure, or Ego

There's a moment in every leader's life when the room turns to them, waiting for a signal. Not for orders, necessarily, but for a sign that the world isn't about to collapse.

You can hear it in the stillness after bad news lands, or see it in the quick dart of someone's eyes toward the head of the table. That split second is where leaders are made or unmade.

I've been in that space more times than I can count, the moments where your stomach drops, your pulse spikes, and every instinct in your body is screaming *react.* But that's when rational optimism earns its keep. It's not blind hope. It's not rose-colored denial. It's the discipline to acknowledge the storm while refusing to hand it the wheel.

The Day the Numbers Went Sideways

A few years back, we were in the final quarter of the fiscal year, tracking toward an ambitious growth target. Everything was humming along until a Friday morning when our Finance team walked in with news: a data error had overstated our booked revenue by nearly seven percent. The hole it left threatened to derail investor confidence and jeopardize year-end bonuses.

The natural reaction? Panic. We had executives pacing in the hall, account managers muttering worst-case scenarios, and one department lead on the verge of making a hasty client call that would have caused more harm than good.

I remember stepping into the glass-walled conference room, closing the door, and letting the chatter die down. "Here's the truth," I said. "We have a problem. It's big. But it's not unsolvable. We are going to face it, fix it, and come out stronger."

The shift was almost audible. Shoulders dropped. Breathing slowed. Not because I had waved a magic wand, but because I was modeling the pace they needed to follow. *Rational optimism doesn't sugarcoat; it frames.* And in that moment, we needed framing more than fire drills.

The Science of Staying Calm

What most people don't realize is that calm leadership has a neurological basis. In high-stress situations, our amygdala, the brain's emotional alarm system, floods our system with cortisol and adrenaline. That's great for outrunning predators. Less great for complex problem-solving.

Research from the Harvard Business Review shows that when a leader stays composed under stress, it helps regulate the mirror neurons in their team members' brains. Simply put: *people subconsciously sync their emotional state to yours.* If you're panicked, they'll panic faster. If you're steady, they'll steady themselves.

Calm is contagious. And when combined with a clear-eyed optimism that things can be fixed, it becomes a performance advantage.

Managing Chaos vs. Creating Clarity

There's a crucial difference between managing chaos and creating clarity. Managing chaos is reactive; it's putting out fires, fielding emergencies, juggling priorities until you can't remember which is which. Creating clarity is proactive; it's defining what matters most *before* the noise starts, and holding that line when the volume spikes.

I learned this distinction during a major e-delivery launch. At the last minute, our legal team weighed in with a showstopping decision. We couldn't move forward without adding an important disclosure that the customer needed to agree to before they could trigger the download of a new product kit. The new requirement threatened to submarine the entire launch by weeks if not months.

I didn't want to "manage" that chaos. I wanted to strip it down to the few levers we could still control. Within an hour, we had three priorities written in bold on the whiteboard: preserve the legal team's trust, maintain team morale, and leverage alternative methodologies. Everything else was noise.

By the end of the week, the panic had subsided, not because the delay disappeared, but because everyone knew exactly what we were doing about it. Clarity doesn't eliminate chaos, but it can starve it of oxygen.

The Myth of Emotional Neutrality as Disconnection

One of the biggest misconceptions about staying calm is that it makes you detached or cold. In reality, emotional neutrality is not about feeling less; it's about choosing when and how you express what you feel.

Think about a surgeon in an operating room. They're not without emotion; they're just not letting that emotion dictate their hands. In leadership, the same principle applies. When you anchor yourself in rational optimism, you're not shutting out empathy; you're directing it where it matters most.

During a tense board presentation, a colleague once told me, "You looked completely unshakable." What I didn't say at the time was that my stomach was in knots. But showing that wouldn't have served the room. Emotional neutrality allowed me to absorb the pressure without passing it on.

It's not disconnection, it's direction.

When the Room Needs More Than a Plan

Plans are essential, but in high-stakes moments, the *energy* of the plan matters just as much as the steps.

During a multi-million-dollar partnership negotiation, the other side's lead unexpectedly introduced a set of aggressive demands in the final hours. My team froze. We'd been blindsided. I asked for a short recess, then gathered everyone in a quiet corner.

"Here's the good news," I said. "We're still in the room. They're still talking. That means this deal is still alive. We go back in calm, we ask the right questions, and we keep them engaged."

We did exactly that. Ninety minutes later, the deal closed, with concessions that worked in our favor.

Rational optimism doesn't just protect morale; it creates the psychological space to find better outcomes.

The Enemy of Optimism: Ego

If fear is one side of the coin that kills good decision-making, ego is the other. I've watched leaders let personal pride hijack a situation that could have been solved with composure.

Ego-driven leadership turns everything into a referendum on status, how it looks, who's right, and who gets credit. Rational optimism has no patience for that. It's not about being the hero in the story; it's about making sure there is a story to tell.

Once, in a joint venture meeting, a partner tried to score a point by publicly questioning our market data. My initial impulse was to defend our position, to "win" the moment. *But I paused, listened, and asked clarifying questions instead.*

The tension evaporated, the data stood, and we moved forward. Had I reacted from ego, we might have blown months of relationship-building in ten minutes.

Optimism is Contagious

The Long Game of Composure

The thing about rational optimism is that it **compounds.** Just like in Chapter 5's Gratitude Engine, people start to internalize the behavior they see modeled. Over time, your team doesn't just count on your calm, they start bringing their own.

I've seen teams go from reactionary chaos to steady, strategic execution in less than a year simply because their leaders made calm the cultural baseline. When pressure came, they didn't ask, "What should we do?" They asked, "What's the clearest way forward?" That's the long game.

Because in a reactive world, the leader who can combine calm thinking with an unshakable belief in the possibility of a better outcome isn't just managing today, they're setting the tone for every tomorrow.

When the Sky Fell at 30,000 Feet

Leadership lessons don't always happen in boardrooms.

I was once flying back from a conference when severe turbulence hit. The kind that makes the overhead bins shudder and coffee slosh out of cups. I glanced around the cabin; some passengers gripped armrests; others had their eyes clamped shut. The flight attendants moved quickly, their smiles a little tighter than usual.

It struck me how much of my own reaction was tied to watching *them.* Their steadiness, or lack of it, would dictate whether the cabin tipped into panic. That's when I realized: in times of uncertainty, leadership is flight attendant energy. Even if you're feeling the bump, you project steady hands.

That same principle has saved me more than once at 30,000 feet in business. During a major product recall years ago, news started breaking online before our official statement was ready. Our phones lit up. Legal was on one line, PR on another, operations in my doorway. The turbulence was real. But instead of rushing out a partial statement or getting drawn into internal blame, we set a deliberate cadence, verify facts, align on message, and control the release.

By the end of the day, customers were informed, partners reassured, and we'd avoided the hemorrhage of trust that comes from flailing in public. The sky had shaken, but the plane stayed steady.

Why Calm Creates Better Decisions

We romanticize pressure as the great clarifier. "When the heat is on," the saying goes, "you see what people are made of." But neuroscience tells us that heat often cooks the wrong parts of the brain.

Under acute stress, your brain's prefrontal cortex, the seat of rational decision-making, literally goes offline. Blood flow is redirected to the amygdala, priming you for fight-or-flight. That's why in moments of extreme urgency, people will sometimes make decisions they later can't explain.

The leaders I respect most are the ones who keep that prefrontal light on. They've trained themselves, through repetition and self-awareness, to slow down the cortisol flood. They breathe. They question their own first reactions. They choose language that calms rather than inflames.

And here's the kicker: this doesn't just save *their* thinking; it safeguards the collective IQ of the room. In cognitive science, this is known as "distributed calm," where the stability of one person's nervous system can regulate the group's problem-solving capacity.

The 2 A.M. Server Crisis

It was 2:08 a.m. when my phone lit up. Our primary server had crashed, taking the client-facing portal down in multiple markets. Millions of dollars in transactions were suddenly at risk. The head of IT was already en route to the data center, his voice clipped and urgent over the line.

The first instinct? Command mode. Bark orders. Demand timelines. Instead, I asked two questions: *"What's the most critical system to bring online first?"* and *"Who needs to know right now?"*

Those questions did two things. First, they shifted the team's focus from the enormity of the failure to the sequence of recovery. Second, they modeled that we were solving, not spiraling. Within four hours, 80% of the system was restored, and by morning, customers experienced minimal disruption.

A crisis is like a chess match with the clock running. The more pieces you can take off the mental board, the better your moves will be.

Rational Optimism in Negotiations

Negotiations are often portrayed as zero-sum games, high-adrenaline standoffs where the one who blinks first loses. But I've found that rational optimism is the real leverage point.

In one instance, we were trying to secure a distribution partnership with a company notorious for aggressive bargaining. Midway through the talks, their lead exec leaned in and said, "We think you need us more than we need you." It was a power play designed to spark anxiety.

Instead of countering with equal aggression, I said, "We're confident in where we're headed, with or without this deal. But I believe there's a version of this partnership where both of us win bigger than we could alone." Then I shut up.

The silence did the work. By removing the ego contest, we opened space for creative terms neither side had considered. The deal closed.

Rational optimism doesn't deny leverage dynamics; it reframes them so the door stays open to better-than-expected outcomes.

Field Notes from a Calm-First Culture

Over time, I've started keeping mental "field notes" on the environments where calm leadership thrives:

- The leader's voice stays measured even when deadlines shrink.
- There's a shared understanding that bad news is data, not a personal indictment.
- Meetings end with a focus on next steps, not post-mortems that spiral into blame.

When these conditions exist, teams learn to bring solutions rather than raw panic. They stop waiting for someone else to steady the ship and start steadying it themselves. That's when you know rational optimism has become part of the cultural DNA.

Closing the Loop: Why This Matters Now

We live in an age of ambient reactivity. News cycles churn every fifteen minutes. Social feeds deliver a constant diet of outrage. In that environment, staying calm isn't just a leadership tactic; it's an act of cultural rebellion.

Rational optimism is the antidote to the default mode of panic. It refuses to be pulled into the undertow of every crisis, real or manufactured. It asks, "What's true? What's solvable? And what's worth our energy?" Then it acts, deliberately, consistently, without ego.

Because at the end of the day, leadership isn't about being the loudest in the room. It's about being the one who can hold the room together when the walls start shaking.

CHAPTER 7: GROWING THE GIANT

From $47 Million to $3 Billion: Building a Digital Powerhouse at Real Chemistry

So *gratitude*…not only does practicing it make life better and more fulfilling, but it turns out it can really help you grow a company.

And you know what? It was truly my first "operating system'. Long before I had titles, budgets, or a P&L, I had a habit: notice what's working, name it, and thank the people making it happen.

REAL CHEMISTRY

That simple practice…repeated in notebooks, hallway conversations, and late-night emails…became the foundation for how I led people, read markets, and, along with Jim Weiss and the other talented executives, grew

Real Chemistry from a promising shop into a massive, modern agency. Fact: People will move mountains for you if you simply have grace and…practice real gratitude.

If you want the short version of the story, it's this: gratitude sharpened my vision, my "connector's code" built the network, and rational optimism gave us the nerve to move when everyone else froze.

And here is the thing: Everything I did before Real Chemistry…every job, team, podcast, and hard lesson…was rehearsal for that combination. I spent 25 years honing everything I had into a fine-tuned personal performance machine in order to become an "overnight sensation" in the 2020's.

Gratitude: A Performance Tool Disguised as a Virtue

I didn't adopt gratitude because it looked good on a wall. I adopted it because it improved outcomes. Gratitude makes you a *pattern recognizer.* When you train your brain to scan for what's working, you start seeing under-leveraged strengths, overlooked teammates, and quiet advantages in the market.

I kept a running list, what I call a "thank-you ledger", with team names, clients, and little moments worth amplifying. That ledger wasn't sentimental; it was strategic. If someone on analytics cracked a measurement problem that made a client's pilot possible, I'd broadcast the credit, pull them into the next meeting, and build the next product around that win. People repeat what gets recognized. Recognition compounds.

Gratitude also lowers the friction cost of leadership. It creates psychological safety. When a team believes their effort will be seen and their names will be said out loud, they bring ideas sooner and surface risks earlier. That safety is rocket fuel in high-velocity environments. Pitch rooms run hotter, not colder. Status reports become truth, not theater. Gratitude is a growth accelerator because it changes the flow of information: more honest, more frequent, more useful.

And in client service? Gratitude is retention. We thanked clients for the invisible work they did to move their organizations…legal approvals, data access, stakeholder herding. When you acknowledge the cost of change for the person sitting across the table, they make more room for you inside the business. That's not manipulation; it's partnership.

Looking Back Now…

I still remember the moment I realized Real Chemistry was no longer a "fast agency" and had become a scaled operating system. It wasn't a single client win or a banner headline.

It was a Tuesday, late, the kind of day where Teams pings pile up, and the calendar looks like a stack of Jenga blocks. I watched three teams, creative, analytics, and integrated comms, resolve a complex patient-journey problem in under an hour without escalation.

They knew the brief, the handoffs, the data paths, and the metrics that mattered. Nobody grandstanded. Everybody shipped. That's when it hit me: the growth story wasn't just about revenue; it was about **repeatability**, turning intelligence into muscle memory and culture into a competitive advantage.

When I joined the company that would become Real Chemistry, we were already unconventional. We had biotech roots and a taste for complexity. Over two decades, we would grow, rebrand, and rewire, through cycles of investment, acquisition, and integration, until we were sitting with the world's largest life sciences companies, not as a vendor but as a **partner** helping them understand, reach, and engage patients and professionals with AI-powered insight, idea-driven experiences, and measurable commercial impact.

That arc, the long build from specialist shop to category-defining platform, is the spine of this chapter.

The story Arc: From W2O to Real Chemistry

Our evolution was never accidental. We were founded as WeissComm Partners, restructured into W2O Group, and, after years of adding capabilities where the market gaps were widest, rebadged as Real Chemistry in 2021.

The name fit the ambition: create real chemistry between people and the brands built to change their lives. Success meant we had to deliver **integration** (communications + med affairs + activation + advertising) on top of real, proprietary **intelligence** (data science, analytics, and later AI) and then operationalize it at scale so the quality didn't dilute as we grew.

The moments that mattered were often inflection points where the easy option was "protect the core." We chose to **expand the core** instead. We pushed into medical communications and provider engagement, added value-based care and market access expertise, and built a data capability that let us map the conversations that actually matter to patients, HCPs, payers, and policy makers, then predict where those conversations were headed.

In 2021, we consolidated under a single brand, Real Chemistry, so our clients could more easily access the full stack of what we'd built. That shift, paired with AI-enabled tools and a SaaS layer designed to be LLM-agnostic, is how our **platform** got sticky across the enterprise.

By 2024, while parts of the sector were wobbling, we grew roughly 12% to about $665 million in fees, with a single acquisition (Avant Healthcare) to deepen med education and HCP communications, because the engine we'd built was resilient. Strategy wasn't living in a slide; it was living in our cadences, tools, and talent.

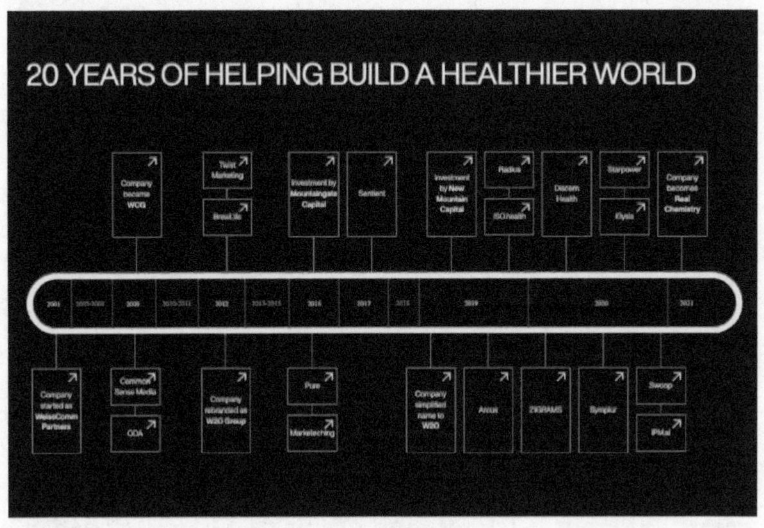

What we actually built (and why it worked)

From the outside, it's easy to see our growth in revenue milestones or headcount. Inside, the work looked like this:

- **AI-powered insights and connected data** to make each brief smarter: patient journeys, HCP influence maps, segmentation that predicts behavior, and precision digital targeting tied to outcomes that CFOs understand.
- **Integrated comms + med + creative** so a single story could move seamlessly from scientific congress to TikTok, from MSL decks to connected TV, from listening signals to ambassador programs.
- **A 360° operating model** where integrated communications remained the largest part of the

business, but with medical communications, activation, and advertising as equal citizens, supported by the strongest earned-media bench and analytics capability in the category.

- **A culture of builders**, reinforced by communities like our biweekly AI "Guild" and convenings like "AI-Palooza," so the best ideas didn't bottleneck at the top.

The test was simple: **did this make us better at connecting the therapy to the humans who need it?** When we could answer "yes" and show the lift, diagnosis rates, adherence, access, and script-to-fill, we earned the right to scale.

"As Real Chemistry picked up speed, I had a front-row seat. I knew of Jim Weiss, and eventually I served on an advisory board as the firm sprinted from "promising" to "powerhouse." Inside that velocity, acquisitions, integrations, and private-equity timelines, I watched Aaron carry the messenger role with grace under pressure. When the stakes were high, he didn't reach for spin. He brought facts, found the small but real wins, and kept people moving. PE doesn't fool around; neither did he. But he also didn't scorch the earth. Bridges stayed intact.

My respect deepened in a harder season. In the wake of George Floyd's murder, many companies issued statements; fewer held space. Aaron did both, centering dignity, inviting voices, and making room for the conversation to be human, not performative.

He is relentlessly fair. Gender equity, LGBTQ+ inclusion, who gets airtime, who gets access, he does the contemporary leadership work when the room is tense. In an industry that can skew "bro-y," he sets a bigger table and actually listens." ***- Jane Sarasohn-Kahn***

What Else Did I Bring to the Party?

Build Value by Building Belonging

If gratitude were my operating system, the Connector's Gift was my distribution. I'm wired to connect: ideas to people, people to people, and then that mesh to opportunities. Over time, I turned that instinct into a philosophy…the Connector's Code…built on a few simple rules:

1. Make the intro before you're asked.
2. Send context with the connection so both sides know why it matters.

3. Keep no ledger. The network pays you back in unexpected ways.

4. Curate for quality; protect people's time like it's your own.

5. After the intro, step out of the way. Let the value happen.

That code shaped Real Chemistry's growth in a hundred ways you can't easily plot on a slide. It's visible in the analysts who became product managers because I connected their curiosity with a client's data problem; in the creative director who found her best strategist because I spotted a "shared obsession" between them; in the clients who shared budgets because we brought their teams together around a common metric instead of a common meeting.

People talk about networks like they're self-generating. They're not. Networks are stewarded. You have to mow the lawn…tend the edges, remove the weeds, encourage cross-pollination. I did that with dinners, group texts, and my podcast, which became a magnet for generous thinkers across marketing, health, and technology.

The show wasn't a vanity project; it was a community engine. Guests became collaborators, collaborators became partners, and partners brought problems that forced us to build new capabilities. Growth followed the connections.

Inside the company, the Connector's Code translated to org design. We cut silos and built squads around outcomes: creatives, analysts, engineers, and account leads sitting in the same sprint cycles, looking at the same dashboards, incentivized by the same client results.

Connectors live for that moment when a data scientist finds a story a filmmaker can tell. Those moments became our signature.

Rational Optimism: Calm Speed in a Reactive World

If gratitude revealed what worked and the Connector's Gift assembled the people, rational optimism set the pace. Optimism without discipline is denial; discipline without optimism is paralysis. Rational optimism sits in the middle: accept reality fast, and choose useful beliefs anyway.

When markets turned noisy…new platforms rising and falling, regulations shifting, healthcare systems reorganizing…I avoided two traps: cynicism ("everything is broken") and cheerleading ("everything is amazing"). Rational optimism is a practice more than a personality trait. Here's how I ran it:

- **Assume change is constant.** If the landscape shifts weekly, build processes that flex weekly. Sprints, not quarters, for experiments.
- **Hunt for the signal.** We built small intelligence loops, customer interviews, platform telemetry, and creative tests, to separate trend from distraction.

- **Scenario plan in the open.** Show the team three possible futures and the triggers for each. Uncertainty shrinks when everyone knows the decision points.

- **Tell the truth about the cost.** Optimism dies when you pretend change is free. We priced transformation into roadmaps so teams didn't feel gaslit.

- **Move when the math and mission align.** We said yes to hard things when they improved outcomes for clients and patients, and when the numbers supported the bet.

That posture helped us pivot from "digital marketing" to "data-driven growth in health," from campaigns to platforms, from outputs to outcomes. We didn't chase every shiny object; we chased a durable advantage.

Everything Before Was Rehearsal

People see a growth curve and assume inevitability. There was nothing inevitable about any of it. What looked like momentum was a stack of learned behaviors from every stage of my life.

Sports taught me team cadence…roles, huddles, and the power of scoring the right things. That's where gratitude got its competitive edge. You thank the blocker because he springs the run; you thank the analyst because she springs the win.

Early digital work taught me curiosity without ego. The internet punished certainty and rewarded learning. That history made rational optimism feel natural: listen hard, test fast, discard what fails, double down on what works.

Podcasting taught me long-form listening. When you practice asking better questions, you become a better operator. Curiosity uncovers constraints. Constraints expose leverage. Leverage unlocks growth.

Mentors taught me the quiet math of reputation. Keep your word. Share the stage. Credit out loud. When you do that over years, deals come looking for you.

Add those threads together and you get the leadership stance we needed as Real Chemistry grew: humble, connective, forward-leaning, and patient with the parts of change that can't be forced.

From Values to Velocity: How It Showed Up in the Work

Hiring and onboarding. We hired for generosity and grit. In interviews, I looked for two signals: Does this person light up when they talk about other people's wins? And can they stay calm in ambiguity? Gratitude and rational optimism, right there. We onboarded new leaders with a "who to know and why" map. Day one, they had five coffees scheduled, each connection pre-briefed with mutual value. The network welcomed them; they contributed faster.

Client growth. We grew accounts by widening the circle of shared purpose. Gratitude here meant naming the stakeholders on the client side who took real risks and helping them win internally. The Connector's Code meant we brought other clients together to learn from each other, even when there was no immediate revenue for us. That generosity paid back in renewals and referrals. Rational optimism meant we didn't oversell transformation; we laddered wins sensibly so the organization could metabolize change.

Capability building. When we had a hunch a capability would matter (say, a new analytics approach or a content engine that integrated with EMR data), we built a "coalition of the ready" across teams, resourced a pilot, and took it to a client who valued innovation. We shared the upside with the team. That loop: notice, connect, act…became culture.

Crisis response. In reactive moments…platform meltdowns, public health shocks, policy changes…gratitude kept the team centered ("you did X last time; we can build on that"), the Connector's Code pulled the right cross-functional brains into the room, and rational optimism set the tone ("here are the facts, here's what we control, here's the next useful thing"). Clients remember who stayed calm and useful.

M&A integration. Growth at scale means bringing companies together. The fastest way to ruin value is to treat people like assets, not allies. We led with gratitude, honoring what acquired teams were great at and used the Connector's Code to interlace talent at the edges: joint squads, shared wins, co-authored IP. Rational optimism set expectations: we didn't promise "synergy by Tuesday"; we promised clarity, listening tours, and measurable milestones.

Culture You Can Feel

Numbers tell one story; a hallway tells another. The culture we built felt different because we enforced the small things. Thank-you notes in public Teams channels. "Name three people who made your week easier" at all-hands.

Virtual team happy hours during the pandemic. Weekly town halls where we met leaders like U.S. Representative, Elissa Slotkin of MI and Katie Couric of NBC and CBS fame, while also sharing client wins. Quarterly "what we got wrong" sessions that rewarded learning instead of punishing it. A bias for open calendars and open documents, the connective tissue of a modern agency.

Those rituals weren't fluff. They were infrastructure. They made it normal to share, safe to experiment, and expected to credit. When you're scaling fast, those norms keep you from devolving into internal competition. People don't hoard when they trust there's enough oxygen for everyone.

Why It Worked in Health

Healthcare is personal, regulated, political, and high stakes. You cannot bluff your way through it. Gratitude helps because it slows you down long enough to understand the human cost of change for clinicians, patients, and regulators.

The Connector's Gift helps because progress happens at intersections: policy and product, science and story, payer and provider. Rational optimism helps because the timeline for impact is messy; you have to hold the line between urgency and patience.

Our best work emerged when we honored those realities. We built platforms that didn't just "reach audiences" but actually helped people understand options. We translated complex data into decisions at the bedside and in the boardroom. We collaborated with partners we once considered competitors because the problem was bigger than any one company. That posture earned trust, and trust earned us the right to do bigger work.

Key inflection points

1) The platform pivot

We made a choice to be more than an agency network. The acquisitions weren't random bolts-on; they were organs for a single body. Communications informed creative; data-informed medical; activation closed the loop. The hard part wasn't buying capabilities, it was **synthesizing** them: shared data models, common definitions of "done," unified quality standards, and cross-functional revenue planning. That's how you go from a group of agencies to a **platform** with compounding effects.

2) Rebranding to Real Chemistry (2021)

Names matter when you're integrating. A new brand gave us a common story and a permission structure to simplify. The internal narrative shifted from "which subsidiary?" to "which capability?" That reframe accelerated client access, fewer doors, and more rooms behind them. Jim Weiss said, "The name 'Real Chemistry' had to resonate internally as alchemic of our teams and our people, but also externally in terms of how we operate with our clients. "We'll always go out to market with a one-company approach. That doesn't mean clients won't buy into a specific area, but they know we'll be able to come to the table with all of it."

3) Operationalizing AI

(not as a demo, as a discipline)

Our LLM-agnostic SaaS layer, our Audience AI capabilities, and the ritualization of AI learning across the company helped us translate curiosity into competence. We didn't tell clients we were innovative; we showed them with precision and speed, identifying influential HCPs, mapping journey friction, and modeling outcomes to guide spend and content. The result wasn't "AI theater"; it was commercial impact.

4) Purpose with receipts: ESG as a business standard

ESG, done badly, is a press release. We framed it as accountability, for our people, our clients, and our communities, with measurable goals (SBTi commitments, a baseline for scope emissions, a plan to transition energy sourcing, supplier-diversity tracking). We anchored it in the idea that health connects us all, and that the way we operate should reflect the outcomes we seek for the world we serve. That built trust internally and externally.

5) Big COVID-19 Effort/Support…It Was Noticed!

In 2020, we unveiled a handful of programs designed to support healthcare providers on the COVID-19 frontlines and provide a needed signal boost to a host of pandemic-related medical efforts. We backed Ventilator SOS, a project focused on modifying sleep apnea devices for use as ventilators and getting them to hospitals in need, with strategy, PR, web design and digital campaign development support. Alongside the California Life Sciences Association, we created a communications dashboard that provided a quick snapshot of media and social trends around the pandemic. We also seeded the #OurCoronaFighters Instagram account, designed to celebrate the accomplishments and bravery of healthcare professionals.

Also, Jim Weiss joined The Commons Project, a nonprofit that created a COVID-19 risk-assessment and mapping platform, as a trustee.

Instagram

#OURCORONAFIGHTERS

ourcoronafighters

Our Corona Fighters

9 posts **22** followers **8** following

We are a community of healthcare marketers and communicators recognizing our heroes during the #covid19 pandemic. These... more

6) We Topped MM+M's 2023 Agency 100 Rankings

Real Chemistry was number one on MM+M's 2023 Agency 100 rankings. This recognition was a testament to the effort and dedication of our clients, partners and employees in creating meaningful work and pushing the boundaries of innovation in healthcare.

In fact, we had grown to work with all 30 of the top 30 pharmaceutical and biotech companies and had a global team of 2,000+ professionals across healthcare and life sciences communications and technology in 2023. This was an incredible achievement.

Here's how the top 100 North American agencies fared financially in 2022. **Click each agency name to view the in-depth profile.** To view all this year's T-shirts, click here. Asterisk indicates an MM+M-estimated revenue sum.

Search

2023 RANK	2022 RANK	AGENCY	2022 revenue	2021 revenue	%age change	staff size 2022	st si 2
1	2	Real Chemistry 1	$514,000,000	$436,000,000	18%	1,702	1,
2	1	Klick Health 2	$510,000,000* (Revenue estimate disputed; see note)	$480,000,000*	6%	1,487	1,
3	3	Deloitte Digital 3	$441,300,000	$374,000,000	18%	1,900	1,
4	4	FCB Health New York	$410,000,000	$370,000,000*	6%	1,469	1,
5	5	Eversana Intouch	$390,000,000	$325,000,000	20%	1,875	1,
6	6	Evoke 4	$368,000,000	$316,000,000	16%	1,432	1,
7	–	Inizio Medical	$352,000,000	$323,000,000	9%	2,110	1,
8	7	Syneos Health	$260,000,000*	$266,000,000*	-2%	801	9
9	8	CMI Media Group and Compas	$253,100,000	$220,200,000	15%	966	8
10	11	VMLY&R Health	$249,900,000	$204,000,000	23%	860	7

Pivots and challenges

Integration debt. Every acquisition creates integration debt: systems, processes, brands, and, most importantly, people. Pay it down fast, or it compounds. We learned to run **playbooks** for harmonizing tools, security, comp, level maps, and performance expectations. We sunset what didn't serve the platform and kept what did, even if it came from a different DNA.

Avoiding metric theater. It's tempting to drown in dashboards. We forced ourselves to connect a **few metrics** to **real decisions**: is diagnosis up, access widened, adherence stabilized, reputation improved? If not, the data wasn't done.

Scaling without breaking the soul. Growth tests culture. We had to keep "builders' energy" alive as the company professionalized. Communities of practice, internal guilds, and visible recognition helped us remember why we started: **move health outcomes in the real world**.

Turbulence in healthcare markets. Regulation shifts, privacy, safety, and an evolving policy landscape kept everyone on their toes. The advantage of being diversified across capabilities and clients was resilience; the price was constant learning and adaptation. We kept sharpening, not just what we do, but **how** we do it.

"I met Aaron in Austin, back when W2O (what became Real Chemistry) was still scrappy. He'd stepped away from another company, so I asked him to grab coffee. By the end of that conversation, I said, "Come build with us."

He did, and helped stand up our tech practice from the ground up, quickly turning it into a meaningful business.

That early tech work, Hewlett-Packard, Intel, others, gave us an edge we later applied to healthcare, which moves more slowly. We learned fast in tech, translated the models, and won in health. That's a through-line with Aaron: learn early, synthesize clearly, and put the lesson to work.

Talent-spotting is one of his superpowers. He knows who will land on a stage, who can actually explain ideas so people change what they do on Monday. As a moderator, he's surgical, sets the tone, pulls the right thread, keeps the over-talker honest, and shines the light on the quiet person with the gem. That's not accidental; it's a craft.

Inside the company, Aaron was our unofficial storyteller. That matters more than most leaders realize. When you're growing from $18M to $177M to far beyond, you're a "new company" every year. Narratives steady people amid change. Aaron thought deeply about what to share in town halls, how to frame the progress, when to celebrate, and when to say, "We're not there yet." I was obsessed with the intellectual architecture and the models; he made sure the humans could hear it, believe it, and move with it."

– Bob Pearson

What leadership looked like (from the inside)

Leadership in hypergrowth is a balancing act between **urgency and steadiness**. My own evolution was learning to slow down the room so the work could speed up. That meant:

- **Decision rights before deadlines.** If the owner of a deliverable isn't empowered to decide, you're running a calendar fantasy.
- **Short, rhythmic cadences.** Replace marathon meetings with daily ten-minute huddles, weekly demos of "working change," and monthly retros that actually kill a step.
- **Normalize "red."** We treated bad news like a service ticket: contain, cause, countermeasure, confirm. Red is a chance to be useful.
- **Coach in private; praise in public.** Skills compound faster when people feel safe and seen.

The net effect was cultural: **we made it safe to be excellent**. And excellence at scale is the only way you get from $47 million to multi-billion without losing your edge. (The exact corporate revenue arc spans many years and ownership structures, but the headline is the same: growth through integration, capability, and outcomes.)

SXSW Was a Key Event for Real Chemistry

Bob Pearson shared some interesting thoughts and reflections on our time together at SXSW…

For nearly a decade, we co-built South by Southwest programming, first with a standalone "PreCommerce" summit to put corporate and government voices on the same stage (before that was common), then folding inside SXSW proper. Our goal was simple: bring the best thinkers together across tribes, tech, health, policy, media, and let them cross-pollinate.

Some nights felt like Texas fever dreams: a dinner out in Dripping Springs, a longhorn in the pasture, armadillo races for comic relief. In the morning, back to panels where Al Roker pushed us to think about entertainment beyond TV while a data scientist unpacked the next algorithm. That contrast, human and cerebral, was the point. The agenda should make your head swivel.

We also hosted "power dinners", which we never called them that publicly, where the guest list was pure mash-up: a Rolling Stones musician, a Facebook exec, a Citibank leader, someone from HHS. No selling. Just a beautifully engineered chance to meet people you'd never meet otherwise. Everyone left saying, "I met five people I'll collaborate with." That's Aaron's networking philosophy in one sentence: make the room valuable for everyone else, and you'll never have to ask for business. People will ask you.

On stage chemistry? Easy division of labor. He MC'd because he's world-class at it, and I worked the wings and the crowd. Ego kills events; clarity saves them. Think of it like Zeppelin: he has a little Jimmy Page in him, knows the craft, but also orchestrates the whole show so it sings. Details like booking the right band for the evening weren't fluff; they were part of designing a peak experience. Everything signals what you value.

Paulo Simas: The Creative Mastermind

"I've known Aaron for well over a decade, call it 15 years. We met building what became Real Chemistry. I was the first acquisition into the company; I'd run brand and creative, later served as president of a few agencies, and wore a lot of hats. Aaron came in as a CMO/VP-marketing type, then ran one of our agencies. Somewhere along the way, we stopped being just colleagues and became chosen family. Our spouses, our kids, we see each other weekly. Vacations, dinners, golf, the whole thing. He's not a "work friend." He's my people.

What makes him different? He's the most WYSIWYG human I know; what you see is what you get. No performative edge, no hidden angle. He's deeply empathetic and radically reliable. If I have a problem, Aaron has a problem, full stop. You call; he answers. And while none of us is perfect, his intent is always clean: optimistic, fair, and aimed at doing the right thing.

If you want proof, here's the story that still gets me. When my son, now 25, was ten, he was diagnosed with leukemia. We were five years into the company, in full sprint mode. Everything screeched to a halt for me, as it should. The company rallied, but Aaron did more than "check in." He stepped in. He filled calls without fanfare, ran interference, asked "How can I help?" and then did it. No hesitation, no keeping score. In the months that followed, when I needed to vent or just breathe, he was the guy on the other end of the phone, steady as a metronome. It wasn't one cinematic moment; it was a hundred small, quiet acts that add up to character.

Inside the business, the simplest way to explain his impact is: he helped make us famous. The work and the growth put fuel in the engine, no doubt. But translating that into brand, into air cover, into thoughtful evangelism? That's the CMO job most agencies forget to do for themselves.

Aaron did it relentlessly, and we did it together. I came up with the name Real Chemistry because there really was a chemistry among the leadership, different personalities that somehow clicked. He amplified that chemistry in the world. He wasn't the "client CMO"; he was our CMO, a thought partner through every transition, acquisition, and narrative shift. When you're selling, integrating, and scaling all at once, someone has to carry the story with integrity. That was Aaron.

People sometimes ask, "How do you go from a couple of dozen people to thousands, from tens of millions to a multi-billion valuation?" The truth is messy: yes, we grew organically; and yes, we acquired one dozen-plus firms over time; we also went through multiple PE *cycles.*

It takes a founder's drive (Jim has that in spades), operational grit across the org, and a trusted voice who can explain what's happening while it's happening. Aaron was that voice, internally and externally. He brought clarity to town halls, to the press, to clients; he created the connective tissue so the company could change without breaking.

There's also a temperament thread that runs through Aaron's orbit—call it calm focus. We're not robots; we feel the hits and the highs. But Aaron has this way of turning down the noise so you can find the one signal worth following. My favorite example comes from the golf course. He picked the game back up a few years ago and, and look, golf is humbling. He has had rounds—no exaggeration—north of 120. Most people would torch their scorecard and swear off the sport. He walks off the 18th green and says, "You know, I had a couple of pretty good shots today—remember that putt on seven?" That's him: find the one clean stroke in four hours of chaos, learn from it, and get back to work. It's not delusion; it's disciplined optimism. In business, that's the person you want beside you after a tough quarter or a missed pitch.

Our friendship sits inside a larger tribe—five couples who are, essentially, extended family. We spend weekends together. We've all seen each other at our best and at our most human. Aaron is consistent in both places. He's generous with credit, ruthless with his own excuses, and clear-eyed about people. He'll give everyone a fair shot; he'll also let go of the toxic few who don't belong on the ride. That's a hard balance to hold when you're scaling; he holds it.

Here's how I'd summarize his leadership in three moves:

1. *Evangelize with substance. He turns work into story without hype. The goal isn't attention; it's understanding that leads to action.*

2. *Create air cover. During integrations and PE cycles, he keeps teams informed, clients confident, and the market clear on what we're building.*

3. *Stay irrationally rational. When emotions spike, he filters for the one thing we can do next—and gets everyone doing it.*

That combination—story, shield, steadiness—multiplies a company's odds of surviving the "teenage years" of growth. I watched it up close.

The last thing I'll say is personal. We tossed around the phrase "chosen family" earlier for a reason. Aaron is that for me. Work will give you titles and deals and war stories. Life gives you diagnoses, kids, late-night panic, and early-morning joy. He shows up for all of it, the same person in the boardroom and in your kitchen. That's why I trust him. That's why I want his book out in the world. It's not theory with a few anecdotes stapled in. It's how he actually operates—on the record, in the wild. And in a noisy world, that kind of human operating system is rare.

- ***Paulo Simas***

Work that shows the point

The work is the proof. Arthritis awareness with a "Chief Movement Officer" in Arnold Schwarzenegger wasn't a celebrity gimmick; it was a reframing of agency for people in pain.

Campaigns for complex conditions, rare disease education, oncology storytelling, and bringing institutions like City of Hope into clearer public view were designed to move a person from recognition to action. Digital-targeting precision and earned activation sat on top of

journey intelligence, so we could point to attributable impact. That's the only scoreboard that counts.

The sale (and the seasons after)

People often ask what it feels like to scale to a sale and keep going. The truth is, it feels like **multiple seasons of the same show**. The cast changes; the arcs evolve. The purpose doesn't.

A sale is a milestone, not a meaning. What mattered to me, and to us, was whether the platform we built could keep doing the thing it was designed to do: help modern therapies and the humans who need them meet each other faster. If the answer stays "yes," the scoreboard takes care of itself.

"Hard Head, Soft Heart" — In My Words (by Jane Sarasohn-Kahn)

The very first time Aaron reached out to me, it wasn't a transaction—it was generosity. A simple LinkedIn note inviting me onto his podcast, no strings attached, just genuine curiosity and respect. When we finally met in a hallway at a Silicon Valley health conference, we slipped into a brother-sister rhythm almost immediately. We're both early-internet optimists who've ridden multiple tech waves—web, mobile, now AI—but what bonded us was the same question: How do we translate all this possibility into health for real people, not hype?

If you want to understand my lens, it starts in childhood. My mother endured a tough leukemia prognosis well beyond expectations because of comprehensive union health benefits, a physician-collaborator, and a strong social network. That origin story made me a health economist with a simple credo: evidence first. I'm open to new modalities—food as medicine, exercise as medicine, wearables that prove their worth—but I want the data. That's a big reason I trust Aaron at the front of a technology wave. He explores early, then translates patiently. He'll use AI to automate the lift—research, drafting, pattern-finding—but he puts humans on the last mile where judgment, empathy, and context live.

One theme I see in him over and over is love—not as sentiment, but as infrastructure. Love is what lets leaders admit mistakes without self-erasure. Love is what keeps community stitched together when the news cycle tears at seams. Love is also what allows rational optimism to exist: not sugarcoating, not doom, but competence with kindness. When things run hot, his cadence is simple and contagious—breathe, name the facts, choose the next best step, go again tomorrow.

My father, a WWII veteran, used to say: hard head, soft heart. That phrase is Aaron's operating system. Hard head: clarity about reality and uncertainty—what we know, what we don't, what job is in front of us. Soft heart: grace while doing that job—respecting the admin, the vendor, the CEO equally; letting other people's ideas breathe; keeping your own ego from colonizing the room. That combination doesn't just ship projects; it builds trust that survives bad news.

Community runs through everything he does. I worry about loneliness as a public-health crisis—the "Bowling Alone" effect at population scale. Aaron is a counterexample. He's anchored in family. He keeps multi-generational work relationships. He shows up for nonprofits and for his neighborhood. South by Southwest is a great example: the health track gatherings he orchestrated weren't vanity plays; they felt like gifts. You got the sense he wanted people in his orbit to experience something together. That's community as resilience—when the world fractures, it's the net that catches us.

I also appreciate his boundaries—the quiet courage to choose good people and release toxic ones. Not everyone will love that. Not everyone should. But if you're in his circle and you earn his trust, the bridge doesn't burn. He lifts, credits, and connects. Those habits compound. They also explain how he navigated the sprint-marathon of scale: sprint for the transaction; run the marathon of narrative and culture so the enterprise can hold weight.

On "designing a future that heals," I hear his voice clearly, and it harmonizes with mine. We both have personal stakes—families touched by diseases like glioblastoma—which makes the work less abstract. The path forward isn't mystical; it's method plus heart. Safer, faster, more equitable care. Data pipes that actually connect. Tech that helps clinicians find ultra-rare patients sooner. Inexpensive sensors and home-based tools so small problems don't become hospital stays. "Small things that add up," as I like to say—if we keep humans in the loop, fund what works, and measure outcomes that matter.

If you ask me what I want readers to take from Aaron, it's this: he combines humility and joy in a way that makes people braver. He tells the whole truth, including the parts most leaders hide, because he knows who he is and whom he loves. That security frees him to be generous, to learn in public, and to keep experimenting without the armor of perfectionism. It also makes him a calming presence when rooms run hot. I think of him as a joyful warrior—courage to be first, wisdom to listen.

In a noisy world, those are rare signals. I've been on the receiving end of his curiosity and care; I've watched him steady teams through turbulence; I've collaborated with him when the stakes were human, not just commercial. If you're looking for a model of leadership that marries a hard head to a soft heart—and makes space for all of us to do better work together—Aaron is that model.

Lessons I'd give my younger self

1. **Be a platform, not a portfolio.** Acquire with a thesis; integrate with a playbook; measure with outcomes a CFO respects.

2. **Make AI boring.** The point isn't the demo. The point is the daily habit, Audience AI inside a planner's workflow, a journey map that updates as signals change.

3. **Choose clarity over charisma.** Cadence beats heroics. Most problems are interface problems; solve the handoff.

4. **Guard the builders.** Your best people are the culture's compilers. Give them space, peers, and purpose, or they will leave.

5. **Anchor purpose with receipts.** ESG is credibility when it's measurable: science-based targets, supplier diversity, community investments, and an honest carbon baseline.

6. **Kill steps.** Process grows like ivy. Prune every quarter, or you'll wake up in a maze.

What Else Would I Tell My Younger Self?

Keep the thank-you ledger. Don't stop when the calendar fills; double down. Build the network before you need it, and give it away as fast as you can. Learn to hold two truths at once: this is hard, and we can do it.

When the room gets loud, be the one with the quiet plan and the clear next step. Credit specifically. Move decisively. Share the stage. And remember the simplest equation in leadership: **people who feel seen will help you build the future faster.**

Real Chemistry's scale wasn't an accident or a trick. It was the natural result of values practiced at industrial strength. Gratitude keeps you honest and generous. The Connector's Code compounds opportunity. Rational optimism turns turbulence into a tailwind. Put them together over years, and you don't just grow a company, you grow a community capable of doing meaningful work at a meaningful scale.

Why it mattered (and what's next)

I've worked across many rooms: creative, medical, data, and client. The through line is simple: **health is personal**. When you connect intelligence with empathy, you get work that moves lives.

The mission that keeps me going is turning a patient's "I think something's wrong" into a diagnosis, turning a provider's "I'm not sure" into a confident plan, and turning a caregiver's "I'm overwhelmed" into guided steps. If an agency can do that, at scale, consistently, then growth is not just possible; it's deserved.

We didn't arrive here by accident. We built a system where ideas travel faster than fear, where data serves the story, and where the work earns the win. That's the difference between a loud agency and a lasting one.

And that's the real chemistry I'll spend the rest of my career compounding.

Lastly, Let's Hear from the Master Himself, Founder, Chairman and Former CEO of Real Chemistry, Jim Weiss…

Success, I've found, has many parents, while failure is an orphan. When reflecting on Real Chemistry's evolution—from an inspired idea to a tech-enabled, data-driven health company serving thousands and achieving a multibillion-dollar valuation—I see two guiding principles at our core:

- *We continuously questioned and redefined what was possible.*
- *We built with a purpose that reached beyond ourselves, inviting others into a shared vision.*

Everything else—partners, clients, resources, even serendipity—flowed from these foundations.

My journey has always been animated by a deep desire to grow, to improve, and to contribute. The idea that "what was good yesterday isn't enough for tomorrow" guided me, not as a burden, but as a source of inspiration. This restless energy was shaped by my roots—

a small Pennsylvania town, Jewish family and early experiences with exclusion and adversity. Yet, rather than hardening me, these challenges cultivated resilience and empathy, transforming obstacles into opportunities to pursue meaningful impact.

Purpose gave direction to this drive. From the very beginning, Real Chemistry set forth a bold and heartfelt mission: to bring life-changing, life-saving information and therapies to those who need them most. Disease is indifferent to boundaries, and our work, too, transcended divisions. This clarity of purpose helped us navigate market shifts, changing technologies, and an increasingly complex societal landscape. We weren't just building another agency; we were striving to become a catalyst for better health outcomes. Along the way, we attracted both people and clients who shared this conviction, forming enduring partnerships built on trust and shared values.

Collaboration made everything possible. Working alongside Aaron Strout, whose emotional intelligence and genuine warmth fostered a culture of connection and generosity, complemented my drive to challenge the status quo and keep reaching further. Our partnership was dynamic and balanced—we encouraged and supported each other through growth and change, always united by our commitment to the mission and to our teams.

Our clients were co-creators, not just recipients. Together, we engaged in long-term, trust-based collaborations, where great work inspired more great work. At its core, our progress was built on relationships, guided by mutual respect and a shared desire to make a difference.

Strong financial partners contributed discipline and resources through two rounds of private equity investment, enabling us to scale thoughtfully and sustainably. But innovation remained at the heart of our journey—we learned from each experiment, celebrated progress, and grew stronger with every lesson. Our story is one of embracing mistakes as pathways to learning and evolution.

People sometimes ask about the source of my drive to keep growing. It's a tapestry woven from personal history, cultural heritage, and an enduring belief in the power of purposeful work. Aaron and I shared a sense of citizenship that was evident in how we supported our communities and mentored others, aiming always to lift as we climbed. His openness and authenticity have been a guiding light.

For me, the essential question has never been about what life delivers, but about how we convert challenges into meaningful contributions for the greater good.

As Real Chemistry grew, our culture became our strategy. We nurtured an environment where people felt seen, valued, and empowered to do their best work—where connections sparked innovation and progress moved swiftly through networks of trust. Aaron's gift as a connector helped fuel this momentum, as he brought people together who would go on to create remarkable things.

If there is a "secret" to our growth, it is simply this: honor your commitments, recognize the contributions of others, learn openly, and never mistake activity for advancement.

I also believe in rational optimism, as does Aaron. This is not blind cheerleading, nor is it cynicism. It is the willingness to face reality, accept its challenges, and choose to believe in the possibility of positive change.

The health landscape remains complex and ever-changing, with persistent challenges such as cancer and Alzheimer's, and fluctuating regulations. Yet, every challenge holds the potential for a breakthrough. Emerging technologies like AI, when used responsibly, empower innovators and caregivers alike. With clear purpose as a guide, volatility can become a source of momentum rather than a barrier.

Leadership, to me, is about presence, empowerment and clear communication. True influence is not measured by titles or the number of meetings led, but by how well we steward the mission and uplift others. As I moved from CEO to chairman, I found new ways to use my experience and network for the greater good—whether through board service, philanthropy, or mentoring future leaders.

Looking ahead, I see Aaron continuing to bring people together and inspire purposeful action as his life and responsibilities evolve. His authentic leadership and deep care for others will continue to be catalytic, enabling others to grow and make a difference.

Success is a collective achievement. Aaron and many others brought humanity and connection; clients brought courage; investors brought discipline; teams brought brilliance and dedication. My role was to keep us stretching toward the horizon, seeing around the corners, and to believe in the power of patient purpose as our greatest advantage.

When you bring these elements together, you do not find inevitability, but the reward of shared effort: Real Chemistry, *built with intention and vision. For any leader, the message is clear—choose a purpose that inspires you even on the hardest days, find partners who broaden your perspective, and foster a culture where everyone is proud to be part of the journey. Do this, through every mistake and milestone, and over time you will build something that truly matters—for the right reasons, and at a scale that makes a difference.*

CHAPTER 8:
THE FIRST TO TRY

Lessons from Three Decades of Technology Adoption

I've always believed that someone has to go first. Not because it's glamorous. Not because it makes headlines. But because without early adopters, without people willing to take that first swing at the unknown, *the future never gets its test run.*

The first time I realized I had this in me…the itch to try before everyone else…I was sitting in an office that still smelled like printer toner and coffee from a Mr. Coffee machine that had seen better days.

The internet was something most people "checked" like you'd check your voicemail: occasionally, cautiously, and never assuming it was essential. But I was staring at a screen that flickered with possibility. A new tool. A new connection. And something in me just knew: "I need to see what this can do before the world decides whether it matters."

Over the years, that instinct would become my quiet compass.

I've been called a lot of things over the years: early adopter, tech whisperer, the guy who jumps off the bridge first to see if there's water below. Some people say it with admiration, others with a smirk, and sometimes with a bit of disbelief. But here's the truth: being the first to try is not about chasing shiny objects. It's about developing a kind of radar, a sense for when something new has the potential to fundamentally shift the way we work, live, and connect.

That radar isn't born overnight. It's shaped by three decades of experiments, late nights in front of glowing screens, and yes…more than a few failures. But when it works, it's magic. You find yourself standing in a quiet moment that you know, deep down, will one day be crowded with everyone else trying to catch up.

Nature vs. nurture: how I learned to leap

I grew up between analog and digital…doodling on my dad's punch cards and watching him dial into remote databases on a 9.6-baud modem by the fireplace. My mother's family hosted a Norwegian exchange student, Inger, in the '60s; at four years old, I flew to Norway.

Early exposure to other cultures widened my aperture and lowered my fear of new things. Later, I chose Russian studies because I sensed a window opening with Gorbachev.

That's my recipe for visionary thinking: broaden your lens on purpose, study history for analogs, and practice small leaps so bigger ones don't paralyze you.

A Seat at the Table: Zuckerberg and the Power of Proximity

One of the clearest lessons I learned about proximity and credibility came at South by Southwest in 2008.

Mark Zuckerberg had just done a keynote that didn't land well. Facebook was still young, still misunderstood, and there were serious questions swirling about transparency, intent, and responsibility. The interview he gave felt shallow to a lot of people, and the backlash was immediate, especially on Twitter, which was still finding its own voice as a real-time feedback engine.

The next day, through a small and informal gathering organized by Robert Scoble, I found myself in a coffee shop in Austin with about 150 bloggers and early social media voices, and Mark Zuckerberg standing in front of us, taking unscripted questions.

I asked him a question about transparency. I don't think I got a great answer. But that wasn't the point.

The point was this: I was there.

I wasn't a household name. I wasn't a tech celebrity. But I had put in enough work, built enough relationships, and stayed close enough to the conversation that I earned a seat in the room when it mattered. That moment crystallized something for me. Influence isn't about status;

it's about showing up consistently where ideas are forming, before they harden into doctrine.

When the Universe Aligns: Foursquare, Gowalla, and Timing It Right

A few years later, I experienced that alignment again, this time with location-based marketing.

In 2011, after writing *Location-Based Marketing for Dummies*, I found myself sitting late one night at the Driskill Hotel in Austin with Dennis Crowley (Foursquare) and Josh Williams (Gowalla). Two fierce competitors. Two pioneers. And there we were, having drinks, talking openly, trading ideas.

It felt surreal.

For two years, my co-author and I had studied these platforms obsessively. We wrote about them. We interviewed their founders. We predicted their impact. And suddenly, we were face-to-face with the people shaping the future we'd been analyzing from afar.

That night felt like validation, not ego validation, but confirmation that the work mattered. That if you stay curious long enough, grind hard enough, and pay attention to the right signals, the universe sometimes closes the loop.

What's fascinating in hindsight is how that story ended.

Gowalla was acquired by Facebook and quietly absorbed. Foursquare survived, split into multiple products, and still exists, but never became the giant many of us predicted. At the same time, technologies I once dismissed, like QR codes, came roaring back years later, finding their moment when conditions finally aligned.

That taught me another enduring lesson: **being early doesn't guarantee being right**.

Some technologies are full steps forward. Others are half steps, waiting for the world to catch up. The challenge isn't predicting what's flashy; it's understanding what's fundamentally useful to human behavior, over time.

Why Experience Still Matters

When people ask what qualifies me to help others navigate what's coming next, my answer is simple: I've lived through the cycles.

I've seen platforms rise and fall. I've watched ideas get dismissed, resurrected, and normalized. I've made bets that paid off, and bets that didn't. That perspective isn't theoretical. It's earned.

History really does repeat itself. Most people just haven't been around long enough to recognize the pattern.

If this book does anything, I hope it helps people skip steps, not by chasing shortcuts, but by learning from someone who's already walked through the fog. Technology will keep changing. Tools will come and go.

But the principles, the human ones, are remarkably consistent.

Curiosity. Discernment. Timing. And the courage to step into rooms before you feel ready.

Those have never gone out of style.

Example: Why I started podcasting, and what I was really doing

In 2006, I launched the *WE Show* to support a crowdsourced-book project called *We Are Smarter Than Me.* The show gave me something more valuable than downloads: permission to build relationships with people whose names could lift an unknown brand.

I learned quickly that a podcast invite opened doors others couldn't: most guests said yes because the medium felt novel, and those intimate conversations created real ties.

That pattern, borrow credibility, create value for the guest, earn trust, became a through-line I've used ever since.

Copyrighted Material
HOW TO UNLEASH THE POWER OF
CROWDS IN YOUR BUSINESS
BARRY LIBERT & JON SPECTOR
AND THOUSANDS OF CONTRIBUTORS
WWW.WEARESMARTER.ORG
WE
ARE SMARTER THAN
ME
FOREWORD BY DON TAPSCOTT, CO-AUTHOR OF WIKINOMICS
Copyrighted Material

Stage time before screen time

My comfort on the mic didn't come from nowhere. In high school, I did two musicals, *Brigadoon* and *Fiddler on the Roof* and another, and discovered how much work it takes to carry a live stage.

Around 21, a friend and I shot spoof videos on a clunky camcorder and held family screenings. I had no idea I was practicing for the digital age; I only knew I liked making things and wasn't afraid of an audience.

That blend of art and tech is why digital fit me: I could teach myself HTML and Photoshop, assemble assets, and ship.

The Core of Early Adoption

People sometimes assume that I leap at every piece of new tech the second it appears. That's not true. I don't believe in "try everything." I believe in "try the right things, at the right time." There's a difference. The secret is in filtering. I trust my instincts, but those instincts are built on a simple truth: innovation adoption is not about the hype…it's about the signal underneath the noise.

That signal is a mix of pattern recognition, curiosity, and courage. Pattern recognition because you've seen enough cycles to know when something has that early glimmer of inevitability. Curious because you're willing to roll up your sleeves and poke at it before the manual exists. And courage because you're willing to look foolish if it doesn't work out.

Me at 24

Trusting Innovation Before the Crowd Did

If you strip away the hype, early adoption is just a form of calculated curiosity.

People think it's about blind faith, but it's not. For me, it's always been a blend: 60% gut, 40% research. The gut is what gets me in the room. The research is what lets me sleep at night.

Take the early days of video streaming. Most people thought of online video as grainy clips on a dial-up connection…funny cat videos long before they were a cultural meme. I saw something different: **a way to educate, market, and connect with audiences** at a scale print or even broadcast couldn't touch.

But that belief didn't come from starry-eyed optimism. It came from watching broadband adoption curves, tracking file compression breakthroughs, and running small experiments with formats no one had a playbook for yet.

That's the part most people miss. Early adoption is less about jumping off the cliff and more about checking where the ledges are before you leap.

Case Study #1: The Day the Web Walked In

It was 1996, and I was working in a space where the idea of "online presence" was still considered niche, almost fringe. One afternoon, someone brought me a printout of a primitive HTML page. "You can put your business on the internet now," they said, with the same tone you might use to announce you could send a message via carrier pigeon.

That night, I stayed up teaching myself HTML from scratch. Not because someone told me I had to, but because something in my gut told me this wasn't a fad. We launched one of our first websites weeks later, complete with clunky graphics and a guestbook, because back then, guestbooks were the social media of the day.

That single experiment led to a chain reaction. Clients started asking questions. Some laughed it off. But others saw what we saw, and they signed on early. By the time the industry "caught up," we already had a portfolio of digital projects that gave us a decade's head start.

The Courage to Ignore the Eye Rolls

If you're going to be first to try, you have to get comfortable with skepticism. Early on, I learned that people tend to project their own fear of change onto the person who dares to try something different.

I remember pitching an email campaign to a client in the late '90s. "Why would we spend time sending something people can just throw away with a click?" they asked. I didn't argue. I just ran a small test campaign. The results spoke louder than my words ever could. Open rates north of 60%. Conversions that beat direct mail. Skepticism turned into budget allocation almost overnight.

It's not about proving people wrong, it's about proving the idea right.

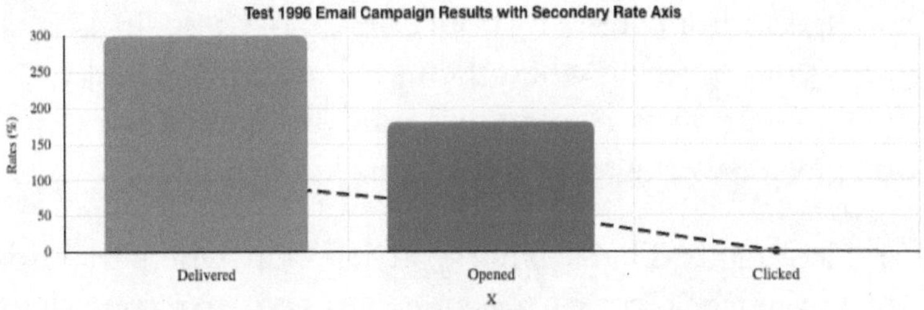

Case Study #2: The Beta Invite That Changed Everything

Fast-forward to the early 2000s. A friend sent me an invite to test a tool that hadn't even launched publicly yet. No brand recognition. No case studies. Just a bare-bones platform and a hunch.

We were deep into client work, deadlines stacking like bricks, and my team was in no mood for "another experiment." But I asked them for two hours. That was the deal: if it didn't impress us in two hours, we'd forget it ever existed.

By the end of those two hours, we were all leaning forward in our chairs. The tool solved a problem that had been quietly draining our productivity for years. That early adoption didn't just give us a competitive edge; it reshaped how we approached our workflow entirely.

Why Curiosity + Courage = The Perfect Tech Filter

The temptation is to think courage alone is enough. But courage without curiosity is just bravado. Curiosity is what keeps you tinkering when the user interface is clunky, the documentation is nonexistent, and the help desk is just one guy answering emails from his kitchen table.

And courage? That's what you lean on when the first version crashes, your team side-eyes you, and your client says, "Are you sure about this?"

When those two qualities work together, you're not guessing, you're experimenting with intent.

Case Study #3: The Social Media Leap

In the mid-2000s, social media was still an odd little corner of the internet. LinkedIn was for job seekers, Facebook was for college kids, and Twitter was for people who liked talking into the void.

I saw potential, not in the platforms themselves, but in the human behavior they represented. People wanted a connection in real time. They wanted brands to feel human.

We started experimenting with client accounts when most executives still thought "tweet" was a sound a bird made. It didn't matter that the numbers were small. The connections we built in those early days turned into partnerships, hires, and opportunities that wouldn't have happened otherwise.

Being first to try isn't always about the tool; it's about the culture shift it signals.

Case Study #4: The Quiet Intranet Revolution

Before cloud platforms became dinner-table talk, I was building internal intranets for companies that wanted to connect their teams. Most people didn't know what an intranet was. I remember explaining it as "your company's private internet" and watching eyes glaze over.

But those who trusted the experiment saw an immediate payoff: communication smoothed out, documents didn't get lost in email chains, and collaboration got faster.

The funny thing is, many of those early intranets became the foundation for the cloud-based ecosystems those companies rely on today. Sometimes, being first to try planting seeds that grow for decades.

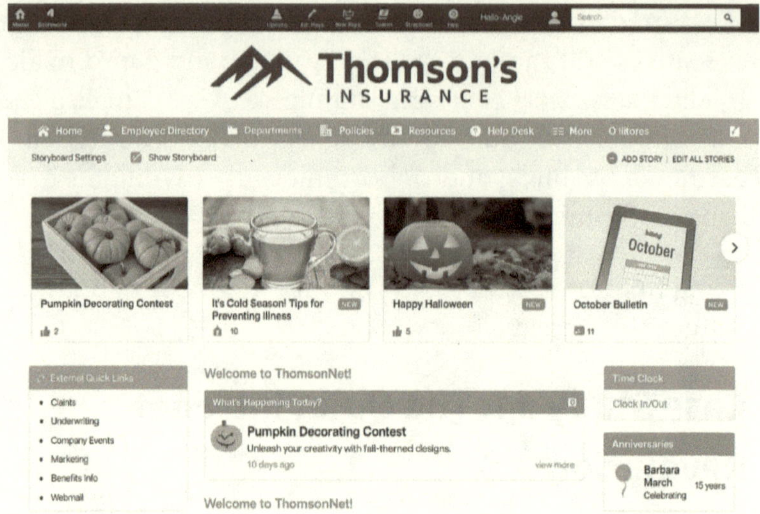

How to Vet New Tools Without the Hype

There's a misconception that first adopters just "go with their gut" and hope for the best.

Not if you want to survive more than one cycle.

My approach has always been a three-phase filter:

1. **Alignment Check** – Does this technology solve a real problem I have now, or one I know is coming? If it's a solution looking for a problem, I walk away.

2. **Durability Test** – Can I see this lasting, or is it likely to get replaced by a faster, sleeker, shinier thing before I've even finished implementing it?

3. **Integration Reality** – How hard will this be to plug into my existing systems, workflows, and culture?

The key is resisting the emotional pull of the "shiny new thing" and looking for the functional heartbeat beneath the buzz.

Predictions I Got Right (and a Few I Didn't)

When you've been first to try for decades, you learn to carry two lists in your mind: the victories and the flops. I've bet on tools that became household names. I've also bet on platforms that disappeared faster than a summer thunderstorm.

The wins are easy to talk about: the first content management systems that made hand-coding every page obsolete, the marketing automation platforms that let us scale personalization, the analytics dashboards that finally let us prove ROI in real time.

The misses are less glamorous. Like the file-sharing service I thought would revolutionize corporate collaboration…until its servers started crashing under basic traffic. Or the "next-generation" email client that promised to reinvent communication but quietly folded after a year.

Those failures were expensive tuition payments in the school of discernment. They taught me that being early doesn't always mean being right…but it does mean being in a position to learn faster than everyone else.

"Answers First, Think in Threes" - Barry Libert

I met Aaron in the mid-2000s, during the era when "online communities" still sounded like a side project. I'd been building community-led businesses since the early 2000s and preaching a simple thesis: there's no more durable advantage than **relationships***—and the networks that are formed and the data that is derived from them.*

Back then, it was called the community, today its' called network effects. Either way, the companies that win are the ones that wire networks of people and machines together and learn from those connections. Aaron got that message of value and growth immediately. He came out of a more traditional marketing world, but he was curious, open-minded, and—most important—willing to unlearn. That's rare.

From the start, I coached him with three operating rules I've used with founders and execs for decades:

1. ***Answers first****. Don't bury the point. Lead with the conclusion, then show the why.*

2. ***Think in threes****. People remember 3, sometimes 7, seldom 10.*

3. ***Keep it simple****. Complexity is a refuge for ego; simplicity is a service to others.*

He absorbed those rules and lived them. Years later, out of the blue, he called to tell me the three still guided his work. That call mattered. Lots of people post a thank-you on social; fewer pick up the phone. Aaron is the latter. He's relational, not transactional—someone who stays in touch, credits others, and 'pays it forward' without keeping a ledger.

If you want my read on why Aaron scales in every new wave—social, mobile, AI—it's three traits I've seen across the best leaders:

1) ***Beginner's mind****. He was willing to admit what he didn't know and reverse assumptions he'd been trained to defend. (I often challenge leaders with Byron Katie's questions: "Are you sure? Are you sure you're sure?" If not, flip the premise and practice the reversal.) Aaron could do that. He left behind "how we did it before" and leaned into community, content, and networks when it was far from obvious.*

2) ***Resilience in the unknown****. It's one thing to say you'll unlearn; it's another to live in uncertainty long enough to build something new. I push people hard—I know that (and everyone tells me that). I've been very hard on plenty of mentorees, and most snap back to their old patterns. Aaron didn't. He kept showing up, kept testing, kept iterating. That persistence is the difference between performative curiosity and actual growth.*

3) ***Knowing when that chapter is over****. Founders and operators often overstay—clinging to a role past its usefulness. Aaron recognized when his long run needed a full stop. Think Federer: leave with grace when it's time, instead of trying to swing on a broken back. That self-awareness is leadership.*

Underneath all of this is a simple market truth I've argued since the 1990s: we over-value "things" on the balance sheet and under-value ***people, networks for relationships, and data/knowledge.*** *Traditional accounting treats chairs and buildings as assets and treats networks of people, customers and employees as expenses—so we chase the wrong stuff. Flip the mindset—treat relationships and networks as assets—and your strategy changes overnight. Aaron* *saw that. He helped build community-led growth before it was a buzzword, and he learned to measure what others ignored: the compounding value of a network.*

People ask me about "gratitude" because it's NOT a corporate mantra, nor is feeling or love. I don't care what you call feelings; I care whether you ***practice*** *them. Aaron does. He's sincere, consistent, and generous. His family has that same relational DNA—I met his dad, a wonderful man. Gratitude isn't his marketing message; it's his habit. That's why his relationships last decades.*

On ***rational optimism****, I'm an optimist who's been run over by a few Mack trucks—major health events, real adversity. I treat them as lessons that I needed to learn. Optimism isn't pretending the bad won't show up; it's believing humans are trying—they're imperfect, but mostly good—and then designing your day to see clearly. You can't get to clarity without* ***silence****. If you're noisy inside, you can't see your team, your spouse, your family, or friends, let alone your market opportunity. Meditation helped me get to silence; any practice that quiets the internal static will help you. When I hear Aaron talk about breathe → state the facts → choose the next step, I recognize the same discipline. Calm is a* ***system****, not a mood.*

A word about ***networks and relationships vs. transactions and money****. Years ago, I argued—in rooms full of skeptics—that networks of people would beat campaigns because communities of people produce* ***network effects****. You can rent attention; you CAN'T own relationships (be it in your personal or professional life). Aaron didn't just nod along; he built long-lasting and enduring relationships. He helped shape programs that respected people - both customers and employees, not just "audiences," and he understood that if you try to monetize a community too early, you kill it. Serve first. Learn. Then create value with people, not just from them. That's how you earn scale that sticks.*

If I were to name "Aaron's Seven," that he learned from me as one of my mentorees, it is the following:

1. ***Answers First****. Lead with the point.*

2. ***Think in Threes****. Decide the three moves that matter, and ship them.*

3. ***Unlearn on Purpose****. When the facts change—or the world does—flip the premise.*

4. ***Automate the Lift; Human the Last Mile****. Use tools for speed, keep judgment human.*

5. ***Service Over Spotlight****. Turn networking into a service; make the room valuable for others.*

6. ***Calm Cadence****. Breathe, state facts, choose the next step—repeat.*

7. ***Know When You're Done****. Close chapters cleanly so you can start the next one well.*

That's not theory. That's how he operates when the cameras are off—how he led inside fast-changing companies, how he treats friends and colleagues, and why he called me fifteen years later to say thank you. It's also why his book will land. We don't need more hot takes; we need operating systems we can practice. Answers first. Threes. Simple. Community as an asset. Calm as a habit. Gratitude as infrastructure. That's Aaron. That's useful.

The Leadership Framework: First-to-Try Without Burning Out

Here's the truth: you can't say yes to everything new. Even with curiosity and courage, you'll drown if you treat early adoption like a buffet. Over the years, I've built a rhythm that keeps me both ahead and sane.

1. Hunt Quietly – I never wait for a press release. My scouting comes from niche forums, industry friends, and the quiet corners of conferences where the vendors don't have booths yet.

2. Test Small, Learn Fast – Every trial has a time box. Two weeks. One project. A single campaign. Enough to know if it's worth scaling or shelving.

3. Share the Map – If it works, I don't hoard it. I document the lessons, show the ROI, and let my team own the roll-out. The win is exponential when more people can run with it.

4. Exit With Grace – When something doesn't pan out, I don't bury it. We hold a short "failure debrief," extract the learning, and move on. The faster you release, the faster you can adopt the next thing.

That's the code. Not a rigid system, but a living filter. It's why, after three decades, I'm still excited to click the unmarked link, download the unknown app, or shake the hand of a founder no one's heard of yet.

Because the future has to start somewhere. And I'd rather be there early, with my sleeves rolled up, than arrive late and wonder what I missed.

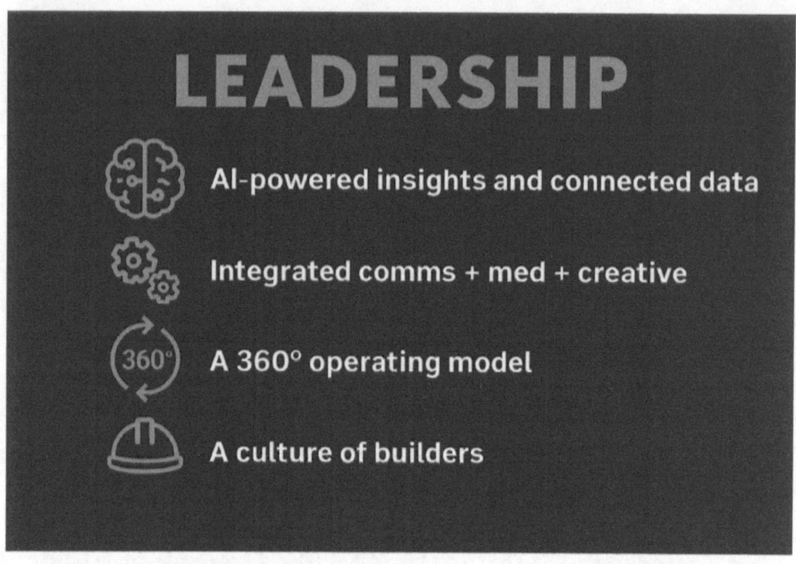

The Discipline of Letting Go

Being first to try also means being first to quit. You can't afford to hang onto every new tool you adopt, no matter how much you loved it in the honeymoon phase. I've learned to set "exit criteria" at the start: if a platform can't deliver X in Y months, I cut it loose.

This discipline keeps you from drowning in half-baked tech stacks and frees up energy for the next thing worth testing.

Closing Thoughts

Three decades in, I still get the same rush when I log into something brand new, something that feels like it might tilt the playing field. But I've also learned to pace that rush with reason.

Being first to try isn't about ego or chasing novelty. It's about positioning yourself and your team…at the frontier of what's possible, then using that vantage point to lead with clarity.

Because in the end, the real win isn't just adopting the right tool first.

It's knowing why you adopted it, how you proved it mattered, and when to hand it over to the rest of the world with confidence.

CHAPTER 9: DESIGNING A FUTURE THAT HEALS

The intersection of AI, marketing, and curing disease

Every decade gives us at least one shiny object that promises to "change everything." Most fade because the effort required outweighs the value delivered. Some become infrastructure.

The lesson isn't "don't chase new"; it's "ship what works for humans." That's the drumbeat of this chapter: take the best of artificial intelligence and modern marketing, wire it to real patient need, and measure success by lives improved, not hype graphs. (If the tone sounds familiar, it's because I've been here before, asking why a seemingly inevitable technology stalled and what would actually move people to action. Different topic, same operating system.)

The most urgent place to apply this mindset is cancer, specifically **glioblastoma** (GBM), the aggressive brain tumor that too often shows up like lightning and leaves families with very little time. I've spent years listening to clinicians, researchers, and caregivers who are fighting for meaningful progress. This chapter is for them, and for the builders, marketers, clinicians, investors, and regulators who can bend the curve together.

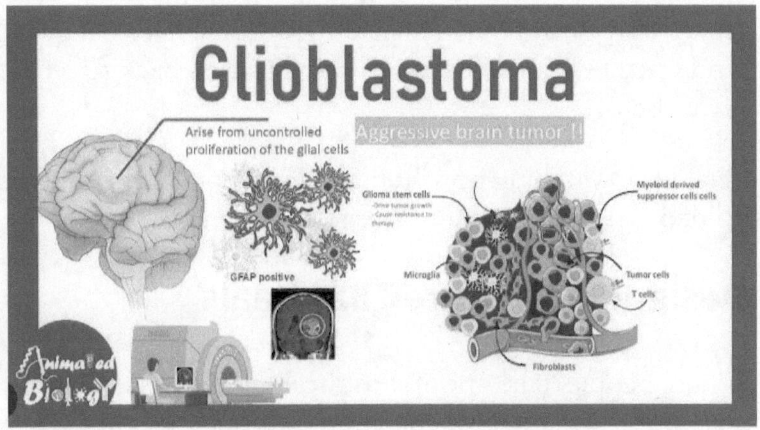

Key Moments That Shaped How I See Technology, Timing, and Trust

There's a moment in every long career when you realize you've lived through more chapters than most people have even read about. When I look back over nearly six decades, through analog beginnings, early digital experiments, social media's adolescence, mobile's explosion, and now the rise of generative AI, I don't see a straight line. I see patterns. I see cycles. And more than anything, I see moments where timing, curiosity, and courage intersect.

COVID was one of those inflection points that clarified a lot for me. Entire industries changed almost overnight. People moved. People quit. The service industry, in particular, never quite returned to what it was. Standards shifted. "Good enough" became acceptable. Efficiency replaced experience. It wasn't all bad, but it was revealing. It reinforced something I've believed for a long time: technology doesn't just change tools, it changes behavior. And once behavior changes, it rarely snaps back to where it was before.

That idea, watching how humans adapt to technology, has guided nearly every major decision I've made.

Designing a Future That Heals

When people talk about healthcare today, they usually start with what's broken, and for good reason. We're dealing with a bloated, inefficient system. Preventable chronic disease is everywhere. Incentives are misaligned. Patients are treated like transactions instead of long-term investments. Add to that the pharmaceutical supply chain, PBMs, pricing opacity, and bureaucratic friction, and it's no surprise that most people feel frustrated, disillusioned, or even cynical.

I see all of that. I agree with much of it. But instead of stopping there, I've spent most of my career asking a different question: *How do we move forward?*

My work, whether through events, podcasts, content, or leadership roles, has always centered on one core idea: **progress happens when you bring the right people together in the same room, focused on the same**

problem. Not people from the same silo, but from across the entire ecosystem. Providers. Payers. Innovators. Academics. Regulators. Technologists. Creators. Storytellers.

That belief was forged during my time as Chief Marketing Officer at a healthcare agency, where my role extended far beyond marketing. I became a convener. At events like South by Southwest, JP Morgan Healthcare Conference, ASCO, and HLTH, my job was to create the conditions for meaningful dialogue, to help smart, mission-driven people see one another not as adversaries, but as collaborators in a shared system.

What I learned is simple but powerful: **no single group can fix healthcare alone.** But when you design spaces where ideas collide, where science meets technology, where culture meets care, where innovation meets empathy, real progress becomes possible.

That insight is what ultimately pushed me to build my own platform. The podcast. The book. The speaking. These aren't vanity projects. They're infrastructure. They're tools to aggregate insight, amplify voices, and build enough momentum to eventually tackle big, audacious challenges, what I think of as healthcare moonshots.

Imagine focused, cross-disciplinary efforts aimed at solving menopause, Alzheimer's, glioblastoma, or other conditions that affect millions yet remain underfunded, misunderstood, or fragmented. We've done moonshots before: cancer, space exploration, genome mapping. There's no reason we can't do them again if we're willing to align incentives and elevate collaboration over competition.

I've been fortunate to spend time with people who are already doing this work at the highest level. Innovators like Dr. Wu at Stanford, who convenes leaders from the FDA, pharma, payers, and academia to rethink drug development and pricing. Entrepreneurs like Glen Tullman have transformed chronic disease management by treating patients as long-term partners rather than episodic cases. Thought leaders like Jane Sarasohn-Kahn, who understand how technology, policy, and human behavior intersect.

Dr. Wu

Glenn Tolman

Connect-Learn-Translate

My role isn't to out-think these people. It's to **connect them, learn from them, and translate their ideas for a broader audience**, so progress doesn't stay locked inside conference rooms or academic journals.

Technology, especially AI, will play a critical role in what comes next. But only if we use it as **human-assisted technology**, not human-replacing technology. AI's real power lies in speed, scale, pattern recognition, and synthesis, helping us analyze massive datasets, personalize care, reduce friction, and test solutions faster than ever before. The goal isn't automation for its own sake; it's better outcomes, delivered with greater humanity.

And if there's one thing I've learned through all of this, it's that healing, whether in healthcare, leadership, or life, starts when we choose to build *together* instead of apart.

Learning How (and How Not) to Use AI

Today, that lens matters more than ever. Generative AI didn't arrive as a curiosity; it arrived as a force. But like every technology wave I've lived through, its value depends entirely on how it's used.

I've been very clear about this: AI shouldn't replace thinking. It should accelerate it. I've experimented enough to know where AI shines and where it falls flat. Short-form synthesis? Excellent. Summarizing dense material? Fantastic. Generating structure, patterns, or first drafts that a human then shapes? Incredibly useful. But asking it to create meaning or lived insight on its own? That's a dead end. There's no soul there. No scar tissue. No judgment forged by experience.

Technology should amplify human wisdom, not attempt to replace it.

Human-first tech is the point

I've always been an early adopter…with a governor. Tools are accelerants; they're not a substitute for judgment. That was true when we were hand-coding websites and blasting clumsy banner ads, and it's true with AI now.

I use AI to spark titles, outline ideas, and draft show notes, but I still write the meat and make the calls. On my podcast, I let software find clips and generate transcripts, but my son engineers the audio because rhythm, pauses, and a few "ums" keep it human.

Tech can do 50–75% of the lifting; I bring it the last mile so it lands like a person, not a machine.

What "heals" looks like when tech and people collaborate

This isn't theory, I've seen the frontier up close.

At Stanford, Dr. Joseph Wu's team can reprogram *blood* into stem cells, then into heart, brain, or liver cells to run personalized trials without cutting into your body. Pair that with high-throughput computing and you compress what took months into hours…ethically, at scale.

On a different track, innovators are working toward lightweight imaging, think "MRI beanie", so early detection becomes as common as a blood pressure check. The pattern is clear: when cost, speed, and invasiveness drop, prevention gets real. Humans still set the guardrails and translate the data into care.

Bridging tribes: Researchers, Builders, and the UX Translators

Breakthroughs don't ship without synthesis. We need scientists and clinicians on one side, technologists and entrepreneurs on the other…and a small but vital class of product-minded UX leaders to tie it together.

The best of them think like industrial designers: left brain plus right brain, lab precision plus lived empathy. They ask, "How will this feel in a patient's hands? In a clinician's workflow? In a caregiver's day?" When those translators lead, adoption follows.

Why marketers...*the right* marketers...belong at the table

Done badly, marketing pushes boundaries and breaks trust. Done well, especially by product marketers, it becomes the discipline of synthesis: thesis, antithesis, synthesis. Think Craig Newmark keeping Craigslist "stupid simple" on purpose, or Jobs insisting that form follow human function. The job is not to hype; it's to make the useful obvious, the complex usable, and the ethical non-negotiable.

Civility with a Spine

We're polarized and exhausted. I try to be the person who can host a civil conversation on hot topics, state ground rules, and enforce tone over ideology, online and off. I've seen hunters, physicians, and activists trade insights without dunking when the room is moderated with respect.

That same skill set belongs in boardrooms and clinics: listen like it matters, argue in good faith, and keep the mission bigger than your identity.

We keep falling in love with personalities and ignoring policy. I'm more interested in pragmatic leaders, often veterans, intel folks, or centrist legislators, who can win purple districts and do the unglamorous work of crossing the aisle. Healthy systems need that tension: principled debate, clear tradeoffs, progress without cults.

I don't want to run for office, but I *do* want to convene people who still know how to build bridges.

From Sick Care to Well Care

If we're serious about a future that heals, we'll flip our operating system: from rescue medicine to prevention, from opacity to navigation, from "doctor knows best" to "patient knows enough to ask."

I'm seeing physician-communicators demystify insurance, scripts for talking to your doctor, and content that gives people the confidence to advocate for themselves, especially those historically ignored.

Education isn't a side quest; it's a lever for equity.

Interoperability is our iTunes moment

Healthcare's data still lives in silos, formats don't match, and useful signals die in transit. We need an "MP3 moment", a standard everyone can live with and marketplaces that make participation obvious and beneficial.

Until then, we'll waste talent and time stitching basics together. When the pipes connect, costs fall, insights compound, and care teams can finally act on the whole picture. I want to help convene that table.

Why Gen X is Well-Suited to Lead Now (But Not Only Gen X)

Gen X folks like me grew up analog, built careers digital, and learned social and mobile by doing. We've seen the hype cycles and the crashes. We've made some money, earned some scars, and care more about legacy than likes.

Our advantage isn't genius…it's pattern recognition plus patience. Use it to mentor younger builders, translate across disciplines, and keep the mission human.

I don't want a chip in my head; I want a calmer, healthier version of childhood where you stayed out until the streetlights came on, augmented by tech that catches disease early, lowers friction, and gives clinicians time to care.

That's the blend I'm chasing: purpose wired through modern tools, not smothered by them.

Why Glioblastoma, and Why Now?

GBM is the kind of problem that clarifies your priorities. Median survival after standard surgery, radiation, and chemotherapy is measured in months, not years.

Yet even in this hardest corner of oncology, real progress is emerging…sometimes incremental, sometimes surprising. It's not a Hollywood breakthrough; it's a set of compounding advances that, when combined and scaled, can extend and enrich lives.

Note: This disease has affected my family in pretty significant ways over the years. So, this is the other huge reason why I want to help with viable solutions.

Technology Belongs to Meaningful Problems

I love tech as much as the next early adopter. But in health, a cool demo that doesn't move an outcome is a distraction. So here's a practical filter I use when leaders ask, "Where do we aim AI?"

Aim 1: Find the patient earlier

- **Radiomics + MRI** can non-invasively predict tumor grade, molecular features (like MGMT promoter methylation), and even immune-related signatures, helping clinicians stratify patients when tissue is limited or risky to obtain. That's not sci-fi; multiple groups have shown promising performance that continues to improve with better data and multimodal models.

Aim 2: Match the patient to the right trial, right now

- AI/LLM-powered trial matching reduces screening time, widens access, and keeps more patients from missing the narrow window when they're both eligible and strong enough to enroll. Studies from academic centers and national groups have demonstrated significant time savings and throughput gains without sacrificing accuracy.

Aim 3: Personalize the regimen; monitor in the wild

- Multimodal models (imaging + pathology + genomics + clinical notes) are getting better at predicting who benefits from which therapy and when to switch. Add **remote monitoring,** passive signals from wearables, and active patient-reported outcomes, and we can catch deterioration early, titrate side effects, and keep more people on the move rather than in the ER.

Aim 4: Make the unscalable, scalable

- Nurse navigators, social workers, and study coordinators do hero's work that rarely scales. AI agents, co-pilots with guardrails, can draft education in plain language, prep visit summaries, pre-fill forms, and tee up the *human* conversation. The goal isn't to replace care; it's to buy back time for empathy.

Tech is the amplifier. It multiplies the intent you bring to it. If your intent is quarterly vanity metrics, you'll optimize for attention. If your intent is healing, you'll optimize for outcomes, equity, and trust.

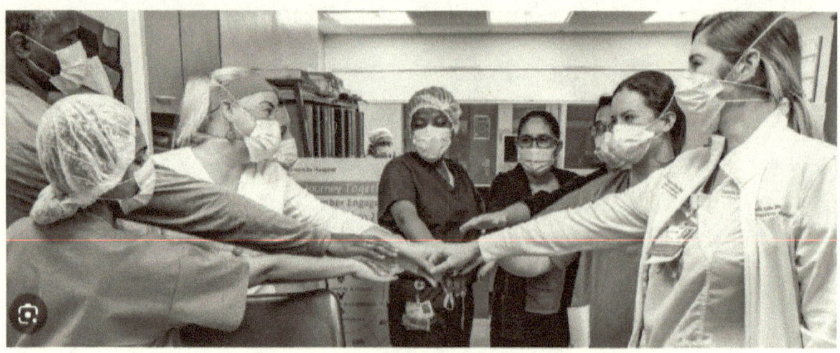

Why Marketers Must Lead (yes, really): Ethics, Equity, Purpose

If you think "ethics" is legal's job and "equity" is someone else's panel, you're reading the org chart, not the room. Marketers are the **translators**; we convene, clarify, and connect. In the AI era, that makes us frontline leaders for three conversations that determine whether tech heals:

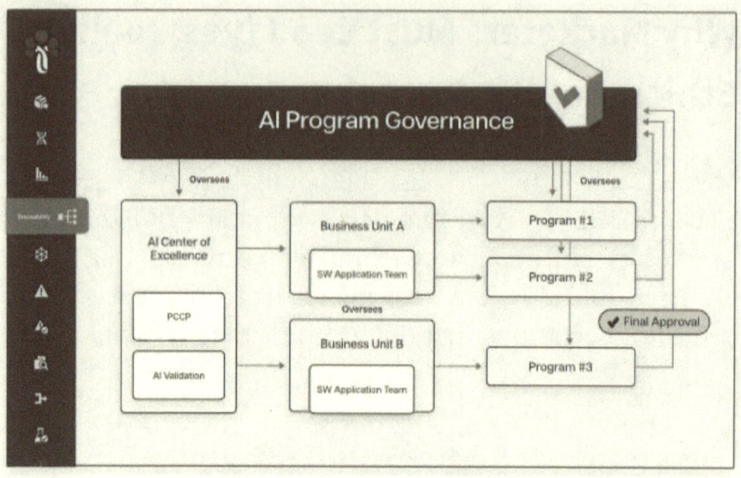

1) AI ethics that patients (and clinicians) can actually use

The World Health Organization has laid out principles for AI in health: transparency, accountability, safety, inclusiveness, and more, recently updated for large multimodal models. The U.S. has a national, voluntary **NIST AI Risk Management Framework** to operationalize trustworthy AI. And the **FDA's Predetermined Change Control Plan (PCCP)** guidance creates a pathway for continuously learning devices to update safely in the wild. If you're leading product, comms, or brand in health, you should know these frameworks cold and translate them into patient-friendly commitments and behavior.

2) Health equity by design, not as a press release

Bias in training data becomes bias in care unless you change the inputs and oversight. AMA's principles for **augmented intelligence** are explicit about equity, transparency, and physician-patient trust. Translating that means: oversample under-represented populations in your datasets, publish performance by subgroup, set up community councils who can veto features that harm access, and budget for deployment in safety-net systems, not just concierge clinics.

3) Purpose that survives the quarterly call

Purpose isn't a tagline. It's the decisions you make when costs rise, timelines slip, or a big buyer pushes for a shortcut. Your job is to hold the line and keep the organization talking like a human. In practice: write consumer-grade explanations for your AI (what it does, what it *doesn't*), publish your performance dashboards, and invite skeptical voices early. The reward is trust, and in health, trust is market share.

Marketers are uniquely positioned to drive healthcare because we sit at the crossroads of patients, clinicians, product, policy, and press. We can make the "hard parts" understandable…without dumbing them down.

Designing for the Decade Ahead: What Leaders in Healthcare Will Need

1) Dual fluency: analog presence + digital leverage

You need to be excellent in the room and excellent with agents. That means telling a clinical story people can feel **and** briefing your AI colleagues (yes, colleagues) with precise prompts, constraints, and evaluation criteria.

2) Evidence velocity

Classic RCTs aren't going away, but they'll be complemented by **platform trials**, pragmatic studies, and real-world evidence pipelines. If your operating cadence can't absorb new signals quarterly, you'll be making last year's decisions in next year's market. (Look at GBM AGILE for the template.)

3) Radical transparency as a moat

Publish model cards. Show subgroup performance. Explain why you chose *not* to ship a feature. Transparency is no longer a reputational nice-to-have; it's how you recruit clinicians, keep regulators aligned, and earn the right to update models in the field. (This is exactly why PCCP matters.)

4) Community as clinical infrastructure

Support groups, patient registries, caregiver forums, these aren't "marketing channels." They're **data and insight systems** that surface side effects faster, reveal adherence barriers, and co-create better education. Treat communities like assets, not campaigns.

5) Systems that center the whole person

The next generation of cancer care will braid oncology with neurology, mental health, rehab, nutrition, and palliative care, supported by AI that coordinates and coaches across disciplines. Build for *care journeys*, not siloed episodes.

6) Ethics that scale

Governance can't be a one-page PDF. It's a living process that includes model monitoring, incident response, and escalation pathways that a nurse can actually use. Borrow from NIST AI RMF; borrow from AMA; build a culture that runs *toward* scrutiny.

7) Measurement that matters

Yes to conversions and awareness. But in health, the north star is **time**, more good months at home, fewer ER spirals, faster trial matching, and earlier detection. Put those metrics on your dashboard. Fund them like you mean it.

The Power of Building the Room Where Healing Can Happen

I've never believed that progress comes from having all the answers. If anything, the longer I've worked at the intersection of technology, marketing, and healthcare, the more convinced I've become that real progress comes from knowing how to ask better questions…and, more importantly, from knowing how to bring the right people into the same room to wrestle with them together.

I am not a physician. I'm not a researcher. I'm not a scientist working at the bench or a clinician at the bedside. And I've never pretended to be. Where I've always felt most at home is somewhere else entirely: in the connective tissue between disciplines, in the space where ideas, incentives, and human behavior collide. That's where my work has lived for decades. And increasingly, I believe that's where the future of healthcare must be designed.

Healthcare doesn't suffer from a lack of intelligence. It suffers from fragmentation.

The people working on diagnostics, therapeutics, care delivery, data infrastructure, patient engagement, and policy are often brilliant...but isolated. They operate in parallel lanes, each optimizing for their own metrics, constrained by their own incentives, and speaking their own professional languages. The result is a system where extraordinary advances exist, yet rarely connect in ways that meaningfully change outcomes at scale.

What I've learned, especially as AI becomes a force multiplier across every industry, is that technology alone doesn't heal systems. Platforms do. Ecosystems do. Conversations do.

Why Marketing Belongs in the Healing Conversation

For most of my career, marketing has been misunderstood, especially in healthcare. Too often, it's been treated as surface-level messaging, brand polish, or demand generation bolted onto a system after the real work is done. But at its best, marketing is not about persuasion. It's about translation.

Marketing is the discipline of understanding people...how they think, what they fear, what motivates them, and how they make decisions in moments of uncertainty. In healthcare, those moments are everywhere. Patients navigating diagnoses. Providers adopting new tools. Researchers seeking funding. Innovators trying to explain breakthroughs to regulators, payers, and the public.

If we want healthcare to evolve, we need better translation between these worlds. We need shared language. We need narratives that connect innovation to trust. We need systems that help complex ideas move from labs to clinics to communities without losing meaning or humanity, along the way.

That's where I believe marketing, especially when paired with AI, can play a quiet but transformative role.

AI as a Connector, Not a Cure

Much of the conversation around AI in healthcare focuses on what AI will replace: doctors, diagnostics, decision-making, and even empathy. I think that framing misses the point. The most powerful role AI can play is not as a replacement for human expertise, but as an **accelerant for collaboration.**

AI has the potential to synthesize vast amounts of data, surface patterns across silos, and highlight connections that would otherwise go unnoticed. But those insights only matter if they reach the right people, in the right context, at the right time. And that requires intentional design…of platforms, workflows, incentives, and communication.

In that sense, AI doesn't cure disease. It creates conditions where cures become more likely.

It can help researchers see across datasets. It can help clinicians personalize care. It can help health systems identify inefficiencies. It can help patients understand their own health journeys. But none of that happens automatically. It happens when people with different expertise agree to collaborate around shared goals.

That's the work I'm most interested in.

Building Platforms That Invite Collaboration

Throughout my career, whether in media, technology, or healthcare-adjacent spaces, I've been drawn to building platforms rather than products. Platforms invite participation. They create shared value. They lower barriers between groups that otherwise wouldn't interact.

In healthcare, platform thinking is essential because no single entity owns the problem. Innovation doesn't live exclusively with startups, incumbents, providers, or policymakers. It lives in the overlap. The challenge is designing environments...both technical and cultural, where those overlaps can be explored safely and productively.

This means creating forums where:

- Clinicians can speak honestly about workflow pain without fear of judgment
- Technologists can test ideas without overpromising
- Marketers can help shape narratives that earn trust rather than hype
- Patients can be heard as partners, not endpoints
- And leaders can think beyond quarterly outcomes toward generational impact

Designing a future that heals requires more than tools. It requires **intentional convening.**

Convening as a Leadership Skill

One of the most underappreciated leadership skills in modern organizations is the ability to convene, not to command, but to host. To create space for disagreement without fragmentation. To allow diverse perspectives to coexist long enough for something better to emerge.

Healthcare desperately needs this kind of leadership.

Too often, conversations about innovation become adversarial: tech versus clinicians, data versus intuition, efficiency versus empathy. These are false binaries. Healing doesn't happen by choosing one side. It happens by integrating perspectives that have been artificially separated.

My role, as I see it, is not to resolve those tensions unilaterally, but to *hold the space* where they can be explored honestly. To ask questions that don't have easy answers. To bring together people who might not otherwise meet…and to help them see that they are, in fact, working toward the same outcome from different angles.

Designing for Trust in a Distrustful System

If there is one currency healthcare cannot function without, it's trust. Trust between patients and providers. Between innovators and institutions. Between data systems and the people whose lives they represent.

Trust is fragile, and it's easily broken by overreach, opacity, or misaligned incentives. This is another place where marketing, done responsibly, matters deeply. Trust is built through clarity, consistency, and humility. Through acknowledging what we don't know as openly as what we do.

AI will only be as trusted as the systems and people who deploy it. Platforms will only succeed if participants believe their contributions are valued and protected. Convening only works if voices are genuinely heard, not performatively included.

Designing a future that heals means designing for trust first and scale second.

The Long View

I've come to believe that the most meaningful work in healthcare innovation won't be measured by individual breakthroughs alone, but by whether we succeed in creating durable collaboration across a deeply complex system.

The diseases we hope to cure are complex. The systems that surround them are even more so. No single discipline, company, or technology will solve them in isolation. But when we build platforms that encourage shared understanding, when we convene people across boundaries, and when we use tools like AI to illuminate connections rather than replace judgment, we move closer to something that looks like healing at scale.

Not just healing bodies…but healing systems.

That's the future I'm interested in designing. Not as an expert with all the answers, but as a builder of the rooms where better answers can emerge.

"Market Maker Energy" - Jeremiah Owyang

I met Aaron Strout in the lobby of an Enterprise 2.0 conference in San Francisco in 2007, one of those hotel-carpet crossroads where a whole era bumps into itself. Web 2.0 was still a sketch; a couple of dozen of us were trying to make a market out of enthusiasm and prototypes.

Aaron was already there, already "showing up": writing, hosting, convening, translating. We shook hands, compared notes, and kept finding each other in hallways, on panels, at his events, and at my roundtables. Those early relationships became the backbone of a decade.

What struck me first, and still does, is his ***follow-through.*** *It's rare for a CMO to stay the arc, rarer still to help steer an agency from early innings through scale and exit without losing the plot or the people. Aaron did. That takes conviction and discipline, not just cleverness. I've watched too many leaders chase novelty and burn out. He chose consistency: keep showing up, keep telling the truth, keep* *doing the unglamorous work of stitching communities together so the next big thing actually has a place to land.*

We collaborated across companies and formats. I spoke at his events more times than I can count. He hosted executive meetings in his office for me. When he asked for help, the answer was easy, because he'd already invested in the relationship with no ledger. That's Aaron's networking OS: serve first, ask last. It's why our circle from those Web 2 days still talks. When you build a market together, you build a tribe that outlives the cycle.

People often label him "positive," but the useful word is ***optimistic with constraints.*** *He's not allergic to hard news. He acknowledges it, then finds the next best move. That calm, what he calls rational optimism, keeps teams out of doom loops. You can hear it in his cadence when a room runs hot: breathe, state the facts, choose the next step. It's not Zen for show; it's an operating system for progress.*

Looking ahead, my lens is AI. I live on the investments side now, so I'm up to my elbows in founders, agents, and applied use cases. Leadership is about managing ***humans and AI colleagues****, orchestrating teams where agents gather, summarize, and decide within guardrails, and humans provide judgment, ethics, and narrative. We don't have a neat leadership rubric for that yet, but Aaron is wired for it: translator by instinct, community builder by practice, clear about when to automate the lift and when to keep the last mile human.*

One hopeful implication of agentic work: ***more analog time****. As AI handles retrieval and routine, we can spend more hours doing human things, walking into rooms, looking people in the eye, building community on purpose. I see it already: demand for trades rising, local groups filling back up, a renewed appetite for in-person learning after the isolation of the pandemic. The internet will feel different when agents fetch and format for us, and that actually* *makes Aaron's playbook more valuable. People will crave leaders who convene, who steady, who make the useful obvious.*

In health specifically, I'm bullish and sober. I've backed teams using generative approaches to accelerate drug discovery, hunting for protein-ligand interactions against wicked diseases. That's real hope. But we also have to tell the whole truth: AI will displace work as it creates value. If we don't solve for ***resource distribution,*** *the "future that heals" will leave too many people behind. We've already seen AI used as a therapist of sorts, with mixed outcomes ranging from access gains to genuine harms. Tools don't save us;* ***design and governance*** *do. Aaron gets that. His instinct is to translate across tribes, clinicians, product, comms, policy, so the tech bends toward outcomes and equity instead of headlines.*

Ask me what advice I'd give a 25-year-old and it maps to why his book matters:

- ***Lead people and agents.*** *Learn to brief AI, critique outputs, and integrate it into a team rhythm while you coach humans with empathy and spine.*
- ***Build community and influence.*** *Public speaking, facilitation, and convening are moat skills in an agentic age.*
- ***Ship small proofs.*** *Two-week experiments with clear success metrics beat year-long visions with no feedback. Aaron models all three.*

I also believe we're headed toward ***health woven into daily life.*** *Imagine agent-guided wellness that actually pairs with local communities, runners meeting within minutes, group workouts tuned to shared goals, nutrition nudges tied to your pantry and neighborhood. (I even invested in an app that sparks on-the-spot group runs, exactly that "right now, with my people" moment.) Tech* *plus human touch. That's the pattern I trust. It's also how Aaron operates: he uses platforms to open doors and then insists on real, embodied connection.*

If I had to sum him up for readers, he's a ***market maker with a human center.*** *He was early to the web, early to podcasting, early to community as strategy, not because "early" is cool, but because he's drawn to the place where ideas meet people and become useful. He plays the long game with relationships. He tells you the truth when it's inconvenient. And when the next wave hits, AI, agents, whatever we call the mutation of the internet, you want someone like Aaron in the room: steady, generous, relentlessly practical, and wired for purpose. That's who he's always been.*

A Note on "Rational Optimism" (and why we keep going)

I've sat with families who would trade every KPI we've ever hit for one more good month. That's the only measure that matters. And it's why I'm stubbornly optimistic, rationally so.

We have proof that well-aimed technology can extend life in GBM (TTFields), can activate the immune system (dendritic-cell vaccines), can sneak drugs past the brain's gate (focused ultrasound), and can train T cells to hunt smarter (multi-target CAR-T). We have trial platforms built for speed and learning. We have AI that can spot patterns faster than any of us and make the unscalable…a little more scalable.

But none of it ships itself. That's on us…leaders who can convene tribes, tell the truth when a model is wrong, design for equity from the start, and keep patients and caregivers at the center when decisions get hard.

Ten Predictions (and Promises) for the Next 10 Years

1. **Agents in the care team.** Every clinic will have AI "colleagues" that summarize, surface risks, and draft, under human oversight with clear accountability.

2. **Platform trials become the norm.** We'll move from one-shot RCTs to adaptive ecosystems that reduce time and cost, with built-in registration pathways. (National Brain Tumor Society)

3. **Consent grows up.** Plain-English, revocable, and paired with community education, because trust is a feature, not a press release.

4. **Equity moves from panel to product.** Subgroup performance is table stakes; deployment in safety-net clinics is a KPI. AMA, WHO, and NIST frameworks move from PDFs into workflows. (American Medical Association)

5. **Radiomics + pathology + genomics** fuse into decision support we can explain, a second reader that earns its keep in tumor boards. (PMC)

6. **Trial matching at scale** becomes so routine that "missed window" stories are the rare exception. (National Institutes of Health (NIH))

7. **Focused ultrasound** graduates from novel to normal in specialized centers, paired with drug-delivery dashboards that quantify BBB opening. (PMC)

8. **CAR-T for solid tumors** adds targets, improves persistence, and moves earlier in the disease course with intrathecal delivery options. (Nature)

9. **Regulatory agility:** PCCPs and good-machine-learning practices let devices learn safely in the field; changelogs become as routine as package inserts. (U.S. Food and Drug Administration)

10. **Marketing grows a backbone.** The best teams become **chief translation officers,** turning complexity into clarity, earning consent, and grounding purpose in outcomes.

Closing Scene: the Room, the Family, the Monitor

Back in the quiet of an oncology ward, none of our frameworks matter if they don't translate into one more walk, one more laugh, one more night at home. Future-of-anything talk should end at the bedside. Are we helping this person, in this room, today? If the answer is yes...because we trial-matched faster, got a therapy across the BBB, extended progression-free survival, or simply made the journey less cruel, then the future we're shipping is worth it.

"Designing a future that heals" isn't a slogan. It's a choice we make every meeting: to aim technology at human problems, to center equity and ethics in our design, to measure what matters, and to keep showing up...calm, honest, and hopeful...until the day we don't just extend months; we change the story.

CHAPTER 10: LEGACY AS A LEADERSHIP PRINCIPLE

What I Want to Share With the Next Generation

The first time I thought about legacy, I was in my early thirties.

Not in the philosophical sense, more in the "What will people remember about me if this meeting goes sideways?" sense. At that point, I measured my worth in quarterly growth charts and campaign wins. My focus was tight and immediate, trained on whatever was directly in front of me.

But then I watched a mentor handle a crisis with the kind of patience and grace that seemed… impossible. The problem was urgent. Stakeholders were restless. Revenue was at stake.

And she, sitting at the head of the table, somehow seemed to see *past* it all, like the issue in front of us was a single note in a much larger symphony she had been conducting for years.

That was my first real glimpse of leadership as an act of time travel. Seeing not just what's happening now, but how today's choices echo five, ten, even twenty years down the road. That's when legacy shifted for me, from something you think about when your career is over, to something you practice in every decision you make today.

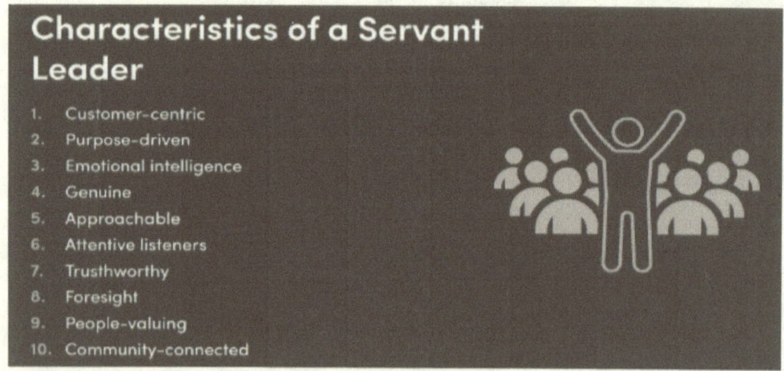

The Power of Long-Term Thinking in a Short-Term World

We live in an era where "long-term" means the next quarter. Shareholder calls, trending metrics, and the dopamine rush of an immediate win dominate most leadership calendars. The temptation to optimize for "now" is relentless.

But here's the thing: when you only play for now, you quietly sabotage the future. Neuroscience backs this up. Studies show that when we make decisions under short-term pressure, our brains engage the ventral striatum, wired for immediate reward, over the prefrontal cortex, which governs strategic foresight. That's why leaders under constant short-term pressure often make choices that look good in the moment but erode value over time.

I've seen companies gut their R&D budgets to hit quarterly targets, only to discover years later they'd traded innovation for a sugar high. I've seen talented managers burn out because leadership treated them as an endlessly renewable resource rather than a career-long partner.

Long-term thinking forces you to zoom out. It asks harder questions:

- Will this decision still look good in five years?
- Are we protecting our values while pursuing our goals?
- Will the culture we're building now still serve the people who inherit it?

Every time you slow down to ask those questions, you're building a legacy.

Why Leadership Is About Service, Not Spotlight

The most effective leaders I've ever met understood that their job wasn't to stand in the spotlight; it was to hold it steady for others.

When I first stepped into an executive role, I assumed visibility was part of the gig. And in some ways, it is.

You're the face at the town hall. The voice in the press interview. The name on the memo. But the point of that visibility is not to magnify yourself, it's to amplify the mission and the people carrying it forward.

I once worked alongside a COO who had a simple rule for recognition: when credit comes, pass it down. When blame comes, take it up. It sounds noble, but it's also strategic. When people know their contributions will be recognized, they invest more of themselves in the work. And when they know you'll shield them from the political fallout of an honest mistake, they innovate more freely.

Leadership as service is not martyrdom, it's stewardship. You're holding something that will outlast you: the trust of your people, the credibility of your word, the trajectory of the mission. If you handle those with care, your influence will extend far beyond your tenure.

A Letter to My Younger Self (and Yours)

If I could speak to my twenty-five-year-old self, the one burning the candle at both ends, chasing titles like trophies, here's what I'd say:

Dear Younger Me,

You think your career is a ladder. You think every rung is proof that you're worth something. I'm not here to tell you titles don't matter; they do. But here's the truth you don't yet see: titles are temporary; reputation is forever.

Stop rushing to be impressive. Start working to be trusted.

The deals you walk away from will shape you as much as the ones you close. The people you invest in will outshine any project you deliver. And one day, you'll realize that your real work wasn't the campaigns or the quarterly wins, it was the culture you left behind.

You will make mistakes. You will take wrong turns. Own them quickly. Learn faster. And never forget that "I don't know" is not a weakness; it's the doorway to your next lesson.

Be patient. Your legacy is not built in a single moment. It's built in thousands of quiet ones, when no one's watching, when you choose to do the right thing over the easy thing.

And when you get there, you'll see it clearly: leadership was never about you. It was about them. Always.

Me…but older, calmer, and hopefully wiser

How to Be Ready for What's Next, While Honoring What Came Before

One of the tensions in leadership is the pull between preservation and progress. You inherit systems, relationships, and traditions from those who came before you. Some of them are worth keeping; others are relics that no longer serve.

The trick is to respect the past without being chained to it.

When I took over a department early in my career, I inherited a process manual so thick it could have doubled as a doorstop. It had been refined over decades and was treated as sacred text. The problem? Half of its procedures were slowing us down in ways that no longer made sense.

Instead of scrapping it outright, which would have alienated the veterans who had built their careers on it, we created a "Legacy Lab." Every month, we'd take one legacy process and ask three questions:

1. Does this still serve the mission?
2. Can it be improved without losing its core?
3. If we removed it, what would break?

Some processes survived intact. Others were retired with ceremony, honoring the people who had crafted them. That blend, respect and reinvention kept morale high while making room for the future.

Readiness for what's next is not about abandoning the old; it's about integrating the best of it into the path forward. That's how you evolve without erasing.

Legacy as Intention

That same principle applies to leadership more broadly. I believe deeply in **legacy as a leadership principle**. Not legacy as ego, but legacy as intention. Starting with the end in mind. Asking, *What do we want to leave behind? How will people be better because we built this?*

The leaders I admire most don't chase short-term wins. They build systems, cultures, and relationships that endure. They balance innovation with wisdom. They know what to stop, what to start, and what to continue. They test new ideas without abandoning foundational truths.

That mindset also applies to personal growth. I've tried to live as an **eternal student**, curious, open, and willing to be uncomfortable. Whether it's discovering new music at a festival, listening to opposing viewpoints, learning new technologies, or simply letting my kids teach me what matters to *their* generation, I believe growth requires disruption, just enough to keep you awake, not so much that you shut down.

Legacy isn't about being right all the time. It's about staying engaged. Staying human. Staying open.

Case Study #1: The Product Launch That Wasn't About the Product

It was the biggest launch of the year.

The prototype had been in development for eighteen months, the marketing team had spent late nights perfecting the messaging, and the sales group had cleared their calendars to focus entirely on the rollout. Everything was lined up for a high-profile win.

And then, a week before launch, an engineer on the team spotted a flaw. Not a catastrophic flaw, but one that could cause intermittent issues for a small segment of customers. The fix would take two weeks. Technically, it wasn't a showstopper. Legally, the product could still ship. The temptation to move forward was strong. After all, months of buildup had created momentum, and momentum is hard to pause.

In the tense meeting that followed, voices were tight. Sales worried about losing their pipeline. Marketing feared the loss of a carefully orchestrated campaign. Finance warned about the cost of delay.

I listened, then asked a single question:

"If we launch now and people have a bad experience, what will they remember about us?"

The room went quiet. Because in that moment, the conversation shifted from revenue and schedules to reputation and trust. I reminded them that this launch wasn't just about hitting a number, it was about sending a message to the market about who they were.

They delayed. Customers never knew about the flaw. And when the launch finally happened, it wasn't just successful; it cemented a perception that the company valued quality over speed. That choice echoed for years, long after the short-term pain had been forgotten.

That's legacy at work: choosing to protect your long-term credibility over your short-term convenience.

Case Study #2: The Quiet Promotion

There's a temptation in leadership to make every big personnel move a performance. The promotion announcement at the town hall. The applause. The photo in the company newsletter. Sometimes those moments are deserved and necessary. But sometimes, legacy is built in the quieter choices.

Years ago, I noticed a mid-level manager in a remote office who consistently solved problems without fanfare. Her team's numbers were strong, but more importantly, her turnover rate was the lowest in the division. She was coaching her people in ways that made them better, not just more productive.

When a senior role opened up, I knew she was the right choice. But instead of waiting for the formal process to wind its way through HR and communications, I flew out to her office unannounced. I asked her to step into the conference room and simply said, “I think you’ve been ready for this for a while. Let’s make it official.”

There were no cameras. No stage lights. Just a leader recognizing another leader in the moment. She cried. He shook my hand. Then I stayed for the afternoon, walking the floor with her, meeting her team, asking what she needed to succeed.

That promotion changed the trajectory of her career. But it also rippled through her team, who saw firsthand that quiet, consistent leadership could be recognized at the highest level. Years later, those team members would tell new hires about that day, not as a corporate HR milestone, but as proof that their company noticed the right things.

Legacy isn’t always built in the big announcements. Sometimes, it’s forged in the quiet moments where trust and respect meet action.

The “Legacy Checklist”

Imagine it’s ten years from now. You’re sitting in a café you’ve never been to before. The city outside is alive with movement, people rushing to meetings, deliveries rattling past on cobblestone streets, the low hum of a place that’s building its own future.

Across the room, you spot someone you once managed. They don’t see you at first, so you watch them for a moment, how they greet the barista, how they listen when their colleague speaks, how they carry themselves with quiet confidence. You realize they’re leading now.

Eventually, they notice you. Their face lights up, and they cross the room. You shake hands, and without thinking, you ask, "How are you?"

They tell you about their work, their team, their projects. And then, unprompted, they say, "You know, I still use what you taught me. About slowing down to think. About doing the right thing when no one's watching. About making people feel like they matter."

That's your checklist, not written on paper, but written in people:

- Did you leave them more capable than you found them?
- Did you protect the values when it would have been easier not to?
- Did you build something that could outlast you?
- Did you give them stories they'd want to pass on?

You finish your coffee, pay your bill, and walk out into the city. And as you step into the noise and motion, you feel the quiet satisfaction of knowing your work was never just about the work. It was about the people who would carry it forward.

That's legacy. And it's built one choice, one day, one person at a time.

Legacy Is Today's Decision Multiplied Over Time

Legacy is not a plaque on the wall or a name in a press release. It's a thousand micro-decisions compounded over time. It's the way you treat the intern when no one's watching. It's whether you cut corners when the budget is tight. It's the email you send in anger, or don't.

The best leaders I've known never announced they were "building a legacy." They were too busy living it. They showed up. They made the hard calls. They invested in people. And in doing so, they left fingerprints on the future they would never see.

You don't have to wait until the end of your career to think about legacy. In fact, the sooner you start, the better your decisions will be. Because when you lead with the end in mind, the noise of the moment gets quieter, and the signal of what truly matters gets louder.

EPILOGUE: IT'S STILL DAY ONE

If I've learned anything worth passing on, it's this: arrival is a mirage. The mountain that looked like a summit turns into a ridge once you're standing on it. The view is stunning, yes, but it mostly reveals more mountains.

You either resent that, or you fall in love with it. I've chosen love. Which is why…even after decades of building, stumbling, scaling, and starting again…I can say, without hedging, that my best work may still be ahead.

That isn't a dismissal of what's come before; it's a statement of faith in what compounds. In this book, I've tried to distill a life of practice: gratitude as a muscle, connection as a craft, rational optimism in a reactive world…into patterns others can use.

But the patterns themselves are not the point. The point is the posture: awake, curious, useful. *It's still day one*, not a slogan, it's an operating system for a life you can be proud of when the lights go down.

Let me leave you with three things I know deep in my bones: why "the best is ahead" is a responsible belief; why humility, humanity, and hope are not soft virtues but hard edges; and why the only title I'm committed to for the rest of my life is *student.*

Why I Believe the Best Is Ahead

I believe the best is ahead because compounding is real and not just for money. It's true for relationships, trust, skill, resilience, and reputation.

When you hold yourself to a few simple disciplines over a long time, the graph eventually bends. It can't not bend.

- **Gratitude compounds.** The more you practice noticing what's right, the more raw material you have to work with on hard days. Grateful leaders take better risks because they aren't operating from scarcity. They mentor more generously because they feel held. They recover faster because their perspective is bigger than the current storm.

- **Service compounds.** If you consistently make other people better, you will never lack for allies. If you introduce without asking for anything in return, rooms open. If you show up when no one's watching, people remember. The "Connector's Code" paid interest for me long before it had a name; it's not networking, it's neighborliness with a long memory.

- **Learning compounds.** Curiosity is a flywheel. You follow one thread because it sparkles, and sooner or later, it ties itself to a problem you care about. I've watched that loop take me from

> marketing to healthcare, from campaigns to causes, from metrics to meaning. The curiosity didn't change; the canvas did.

I also believe the best is ahead because the problems that matter most to me, health equity, ethical AI, and accelerating research for brutal diseases like glioblastoma, are not solved. They're moving. They're asking for new coalitions, new language, and a sturdier kind of leadership. I want in on that work; not as a mascot, but as a contributor who can convene, translate, and ship.

And finally, I believe the best is ahead because I'm less foolish than I used to be. Younger me thought velocity and intensity were the same thing. Older me knows that urgency and peace can share a body. Younger me equated scale with significance. Older me understands that significance is measured in changed lives, not headcount. I wouldn't trade the miles.

But I wouldn't go back, either.

What "Day One" Means to Me

I didn't coin the phrase. But I adopted it on purpose.

Day one means you resist the fat middle of success; the sleepiness that comes when a reputation can do the work your hands used to do. It means you insist on the beginner's advantages even when you're not a beginner: you listen longer, test smaller, and ship sooner.

You come to the table ready to learn, not to be celebrated. You tell the truth about the problem, even if the truth threatens your position. You leave space in the plan for surprise.

Practically, *day one* looks like this:

- **Write the memo before the meeting.** Clarity is a kindness. If I can't explain it cleanly, I don't understand it enough to ask others to carry it.
- **Draw the decision in public.** 4W closes (What, Why, Who, When), a shared log, and a bias to reversible bets. Process is not bureaucracy when it speeds up the work.
- **Make a friend every week.** Not a "contact." A friend. Someone I can help *today* without a ledger. The helper's high is real; the long arc is, too.
- **Stay close to the field.** Talk to patients, nurses, families, founders, and scientists. Sit with their constraints and their hope. Your calendar is your character.
- **Ask better questions.** Not "What can we sell?" but "Where is the friction, who is paying the tax, and what would relief feel like?"

Day one isn't about pretending you're new. It's about refusing to act like you're done.

Humility, Humanity, and Hope

If you take nothing else from my story, take these three words and make them your scaffolding.

Humility

Humility is precision, not posture. It's the willingness to sense reality faster than your ego wants to. In practice, humility sounds like:

- "I was wrong. Let me fix it."
- "You have the insight; I have the air cover. How do I help you win?"
- "That joke didn't land. I'm sorry."
- "We can do better for this community, and here's what I missed."

Humility doesn't dilute leadership; it strengthens it. People will follow you into the fire if they believe you can *see*. They will follow you even more if they know you can *adjust*.

Humanity

Humanity is the decision to keep people at the center of problems that are easier to treat as abstractions. It is scheduling time for someone who can't help your career. It is paying attention to the person in the back row. It is designing an experience for the stressed-out parent on a Tuesday night, not for the case study you hope to present at a conference.

Humanity is also fierce. It says, "We don't use people as props." It says, "No campaign is worth a broken teammate." It says, "If we can't explain this in plain language to the person bearing the consequence, we haven't earned the right to ship."

Hope

Hope is strategy's oxygen. I don't mean fantasy. I mean a stubborn, informed conviction that tomorrow can be made better by the work we choose today. Hope is a choice you make when the facts are gray and the stakes are real. It trains your eyes to spot the lever others miss.

Everything in this book...purpose, practice, connection, discipline...tries to make hope practical. Because on the days when the meeting goes sideways, the deal falls apart, the test fails, or the diagnosis arrives, "be positive" is a brittle idea. But "be useful" is not. "Be kind" is not. "Try again, smaller," is not. That kind of hope survives contact with reality.

The Eternal Student

I intend to die a beginner in something important.

The world rewards expertise and personas; I'm grateful for any credibility I've earned. But the best days of my life tend to start with sentences like, "Teach me how this works," and "I don't understand...can you show me?" Curiosity is a self-rescue device; it drags you out of stale air and into rooms with windows.

Here's what staying a student looks like for me now:

- **Study across boundaries.** Healthcare teaches marketers how to matter. Marketing teaches scientists how to be understood. Policy teaches both how to scale fairness. Art teaches all of us what it means to be alive. Cross-pollinate or calcify, those are the options.

- **Audit my inputs.** Curate the feeds. Prune the outrage. Chase depth. Re-read the books that slowed me down. Read the people who make me bristle and then ask why.

- **Prototype habits.** I still run small experiments with how I work: new ways to prep, to debrief, to thank, to rest. I retire what doesn't serve. I keep what moves the needle.

- **Learn in public.** Share drafts. Admit uncertainty. Let people watch the sausage-making. Perfectionism is just fear with a fancy coat; it's allergic to learning.

- **Ask younger people to lead the tour.** Let them decide the playlist; follow their nose through the museum. They will take you to corners you didn't know existed.

If this sounds romantic, it isn't. It's selfish. Learning keeps me alive. It reminds me that I'm not the protagonist of every story, and that good ideas outnumber my capacity to execute them. That's thrilling, not discouraging.

Don't Be Afraid to Show Your Vulnerability

As I grew professionally, I also grew emotionally. Vulnerability didn't come naturally to me early on. I had learned, like many men of my generation, to compartmentalize feelings. But life has a way of breaking down those walls.

A painful breakup, a period of deep introspection, and even a book, *The Celestine Prophecy*, opened me up in ways I didn't anticipate. I remember sitting alone on a rooftop in Boston in the middle of the night, finally allowing myself to feel everything I'd been suppressing. From that moment on, I decided I didn't want to live armored anymore.

That shift changed how people experienced me. Guests on my podcast began telling me they felt safe opening up, that the conversations felt different. I realized vulnerability wasn't a liability; it was a bridge. It allowed others to bring their full selves into the room. And that, in turn, made the work more meaningful.

This way of being extended into how I work with women, too. I've always felt deeply comfortable collaborating with women, not because I see myself as enlightened, but because I've listened. My wife, my colleagues, and my mentors have taught me how important empathy is in creating inclusive, respectful environments. It's not about grand gestures; it's about awareness, about noticing how power dynamics show up in small, everyday moments.

Leadership is Service

Looking back, what ties all of this together is a simple truth: leadership isn't about the spotlight, it's about service. It's about showing up consistently, investing in people without keeping score, and staying open to learning, even when it's uncomfortable. I didn't always get it right. I made mistakes. I had to learn how to hear feedback without defensiveness and how to take ownership without ego. But those lessons shaped me into a better leader, partner, and human being.

If there's one thing I hope came through in this book for you, it's that none of this was accidental. Everything good in my life was built one conversation at a time, one relationship at a time, one moment of courage at a time. And it's still being built.

Work That Still Calls My Name

I can name the frontier that tugs at me when I wake up…

- **Turning AI toward human problems that matter.** Not as a novelty or a veneer but as an engine…summarizing patient journeys, translating for families, relieving nurses of documentation burdens, triaging with empathy, getting the right trial to the right person a month sooner than we used to. Marketing can convene the people who don't share conferences but do share a patient. We can help build language and bridges.

- **Glioblastoma advocacy and research acceleration.** If you've read this far, you know why this disease lives in my throat. I want to gather funders, storytellers, researchers, and caregivers around a table with a different brief: collapse time. It doesn't always take more money to move faster; it takes better choreography and fewer handoffs. Let me be the stage manager for those rooms.

- **Leader formation that prioritizes service.** A generation of operators is coming up who have seen inside the machine from day one. They are allergic to performative leadership and rightly skeptical of institutions. They will follow someone who is brave, human, and technically excellent. I want to mentor those leaders, show them how to hold paradox and keep grace, how to make decisions in fog, how to apologize without groveling and praise without flattery.

- **Health equity as design, not charity.** Equity is an architectural choice. You can wire a system to include, or you can wire it to exclude and patch it later with grants. The former is harder. It is also cheaper in the long run. If I can help more organizations choose design, I will consider that among my best work.

I don't need my name on any of it. I want to be the person who answers the phone, sends the email, writes the brief, hosts the dinner, and keeps the meeting honest.

What I Owe and What I've Learned

When I inventory my life, the ledger is lopsided. Family, mentors, teammates, clients, patients, strangers…so many people poured into me. If gratitude is a practice, *debt* is a perspective.

I owe the teachers who didn't write me off, the leaders who gave me rope *and* guardrails, the teams who executed like artists, the friends who told me truths I didn't want to hear, and the communities who let me try again after I got it wrong. I owe the people whose lives have been touched by the diseases we aim to beat; their courage dwarfs my complaints.

I owe myself, too, not perfection, but maintenance. Sleep, movement, quiet, laughter. Leaders who neglect themselves become unsafe to follow. I've flirted with that edge. I've come to recognize the tells: the calendar full of obligations and empty of oxygen, the fractured attention I try to pass off as "availability," the way cynicism puts its feet up when I stop filling my own well. I don't want to be that guy. I want to be the kind of human who makes other humans glad they tried today.

Some lessons I keep taped to the inside of my skull:

- **Add oxygen, not heat.** Rooms don't need more drama; they need more air. Ask questions that lower shoulders. Name the fear without feeding it.

- **Choose useful over right.** Being correct is easy; being constructive is rare.

- **Make promises your worst day can keep.** Under-commit. Over-prepare. Over-communicate.

- **Ship the small thing today.** The big thing will require the confidence you build by shipping the small stuff on time.

- **Hold the tension.** You can care for people and hold the bar. You can be urgent and kind. You can celebrate and still insist on better.

- **Tell the truth faster.** It is cheaper than delay, kinder than spin, and the only basis for trust.

What I Want for You

If we never meet, and this book is the only conversation we get, here's what I hope it leaves behind:

- **Permission.** Permission to define purpose on your own terms and then go scare yourself into living it. Permission to build a life you can explain to your kids without asterisks.

- **Practice.** Not just inspiration, but routines and rituals that turn good intentions into good habits. The difference between a Tuesday that happens to you and a Tuesday you lead is smaller than you think. It's a memo. A decision log. A 12-minute stand-up. A walk after the hardest meeting.

- **People.** A hunger to be the kind of person others call when it's messy. The friend who introduces, shows up, and follows through. The colleague who remembers names. The leader who learns.

- **Patience.** A long view that makes you dangerous: you're hard to rile, hard to manipulate, and impossible to stop because you don't burn out every time the news cycle spikes.
- **A plan.** Not a rigid one, but a simple one: What will you learn next? Who will you serve next? What will you ship next? When will you rest next? Write it. Post it. Live it.

And when you blow it (as you will)…*repair quickly*. Say the words: "I'm sorry." "Thank you." "I need help." These are not weaknesses; they are the grammar of a grown-up life.

A Letter to Tomorrow

Tomorrow, I don't know exactly what you'll ask of me. Maybe a joyful sprint. Maybe a hard call. Maybe a quiet day in the stacks, reading papers and making lists. Maybe another call from a friend who just heard the word no one wants to hear.

I promise you this: I will bring a learner's eyes and a builder's hands. I will err on the side of kindness. I will make a list I can finish and finish it. I will write the note, send the introduction, or leave the voice memo that changes someone's day. I will return to the places where purpose and usefulness intersect and plant myself there. And when I fail, I will ask for grace, recover, and try again.

I will remember that leadership is borrowed…on loan from the people who let you serve them…and that the rent is due daily in the currency of attention, care, and results. I will keep the circle open for people who don't look or sound like me, because homogeneity makes teams weak and progress slow. I will praise with receipts and critique with respect. I will keep an eye on the quiet ones, because genius is shy.

I will keep a place at the table for hope.

The Last Word (For Now)

We don't get to decide how long we have. We do get to decide how we spend what we have. If this book has been worth your time, it's because it gave you a few more ways to spend yours well…on people, on problems that deserve you, on work that lifts someone besides your own reflection.

I am proud of what we've built and grateful for every partner who helped build it. But I am more energized by the unfinished. There are patients waiting for better answers. There are communities that deserve more equitable systems. There are leaders who are ready to step into a different template. one that balances ambition with empathy, speed with stewardship.

So yes, it's still day one. Not because the past doesn't matter, but because it *does*, and it's handed us tools we weren't ready for until now.

Let's use them with humility. Let's use them with humanity. Let's use them with hope.

I'll see you at first light.

Aaron Strout

Aaron Strout is a 30-year marketing leader, connector, and author of Wired for Purpose: Why Humanity Is the Biggest Differentiation in a Digital World. Known for bringing humanity to innovation, he has led at the intersection of technology, marketing, and leadership across roles at Real Chemistry, Mzinga and Fidelity. A keynote speaker, podcast host, advisor, and mentor, Aaron helps people and organizations thrive through meaningful connection.

He lives in the Bay Area with his wife, Melanie and is a huge fan of Boston sports, BBQ and long walks with his dogs, Bender and Roo. Find out more at: www.wiredforpurpose.com

www.ingramcontent.com/pod-product-compliance
Lightning Source LLC
La Vergne TN
LVHW100525110826
845146LV00002B/775